A destiny : Stefanie Powers

By KAY J. WAGNER

To my sun, Vince.

CONTENTS

Chapter 1 : Childhood in Hollywood

Stefanie Powers (her reel name Stefania Zofia Federkiewicz) was born on November 2, 1942 in Hollywood, Los Angeles, California. Of Polish origin, her ancestors immigrated to the United States during the first part of the 20th century.

His mother Julianna Dimitria Golan, was born on July 21, 1912 on the family farm near Middletown, New York. She is the daughter of Zofja and Frederick Golan. The family lives in the country and the family's uncle, Leo teaches them English through geographical magazines. Rural America sees the arrival of the telephone and the advertisements feature young girls walking around in beautiful cars. The countryside provided them with an idyllic childhood, but the two sisters grew up dreaming of musical films.

Julianna and Helena Golan left the family farm in Upstate New York at the age of eighteen and both moved to The City of

Lights: New York not far from Central Park in a small family boarding house run by an Italian woman : Carmela.

Julianna and Helena Golan want to work in theatre and music films. They show up at auditions while working as hostesses in a small cinema on 57th Street called the Carnegie Small Theatre. It is a very glamorous cinema that serves cocktails, tea and coffee and is the only place in the city where foreign films are screened.

In 1934, Julianna Golan travelled to Hollywood by boat via the Panama Canal and settled in « Lido Hotel » located north of Hollywood Boulevard, not far from a popular spot : Montecito, near Santa Barbara.

Hollywood Boulevard is synonymous with the film industry that stretches from Sunset Boulevard west of Laurel Canyon to Prospect Avenue when the city of Hollywood is annexed to Los Angeles, some 20 years later. Grand establishments such as: El Capitan Theatre, Pantages Theatre, Warner Brothers Theatre, Chinese Theatre already attract visitors and celebrities.

Actors, directors, writers all gather in town for dinner or a drink at the « Grill Musso & Frank ». Pimps and prostitutes have not yet taken possession of the premises and Hollywood Boulevard remains the perfect place for a walk.

In the lobby of the "Lido Hotel", a pianist plays in the evening at cocktail time. Julianna Golan meets a young photographer who would become her first husband : Paul Morrison Bloomfield. She abandons her artistic dreams for marriage and motherhood. They will have a son : Jeffrey, then a daughter: Stefanie. The couple divorced when Stefanie was just seven years old. She will rarely talk about her father.

Julianna Golan is a devoted mom to her two children and never dries up on stories to tell them every day. She is totally dedicated to them and communicates to them the values of effort and work. She is also the stable part of the home and Stefanie Powers remembers times when sometimes her mother went to a party. She still remembers her black silk dress rustling when she was moving and the perfume she wore for these special occasions: Shalimar. These same memories and scents of childhood that one keeps all one's life.

The family world is small and the rest of her family is settled in the eastern United States, while Stefanie Powers and her parents live in California. Her mother's sister, her aunt Helena lives not far from them, she is married to Uncle Howard who is a former comedian who practiced in cabarets. He is a tall and robust man of a joyful nature. He then became Casting Director for the Television Studios and later joined Technicolor. He teaches Stefanie to dance to a song « The Sunny Side of the Street », which she has very fond memories of.

It was also the time of the vendors who crisscrossed every neighborhood, every street to present their items for sale, be it encyclopedias or vacuum cleaners. His upbringing mirrors the fifties when religion occupied its place in the family.

Each week, the family attends Reverend Norman's sermon. At home the children speak English and Polish. Her brother Jeff and their friends form a small group that comes together to share the same games of young people their age.

In their neighbourhood near their home there was a family whose father was French and the Italian mother: the Bagier family. The father was the son of a countess called « Mara » who was famous in the fashion world for his shirts, ties and accessories. The family had lived in Puerto Rico where their two children, their son Robin and their daughter Mara were born.

Stefanie and her brother Jeff and the two Bagier children together are a group of young people who get along well. A little later, a family friend Paul Kohner who is an agent in Hollywood will be regularly invited to their table. Her daughter Susan, is a young film hopeful, she starred in a film alongside Lana Turner and Sandra Dee. A few years later, Sefanie Powers co-starred with Lana Turner and Sandra Dee.

Julianna Golan meets Jack Robinson. Tall, robust and like John Wayne, he will arrive like a wave in their lives and will be the only father figure for Stefanie Powers. Uncle Jack breeds thoroughbreds, drives a Cadillac Eldorado and a Mercedes 300 with a horse's head on the bonnet.

At their ranch in Circle Jr. in California, there are

thoroughbred horses that are bred to be auctioned off to buyers. There are also monkeys, goats and young lambs. Jeff and Stefanie Powers grow up surrounded by animals on their ranch.

At the time, the population of Los Angeles was just over two million people. A Russian ballet by the Diaghilev company of Monte Carlo was touring America, its stage manager Michael Panieff was the soloist when the Second World War broke out in Europe.

Then, on the other side of the Atlantic, it was the attack on Pearl Harbor and the American Congress declared war on Japan. Micha Panieff was recruited into the army and left to join a tank corps. He then returned to France and opened a dance school on the French Riviera.

Stefanie Powers joins a ballet class in Hollywood. In her class, there are two other young girls: Natalie Wood who was a little older and was already a child star. She became Robert Wagner's first and second wife. The second, Jill Openheimer (Jill St John) will become Robert Wagner's fourth wife in the city. As for Stefanie Powers, she will be Mrs. Jonathan Hart (the wife of Robert Wagner) on television in the series « Hart to Hart ».

Sometimes later, Natalie Wood left ballet to start her future acting career.

At the age of fourteen, Stefanie grew rapidly to reach her adult size. Her body changes and changes with adolescence. A dancer choreographer from New York, Eugene Loring, set up an American dance school « American School of Dance » on Hollywood Boulevard. This course has become the focal point for modern dance on the West Coast of the United States by recruiting the best teachers and dancers.

Stefanie Powers joins one of the dance classes her teacher Matt Mattox introduces to contemporary dance. In the hall of the dance school are displayed the requests of dancers for productions of television series and films, allowing the dancers to appear at auditions and land roles, whether in film or television.

At just 15 years old, Stefanie Powers began auditioning with a friend Kathy Gale who was a little older than her. Their mothers knew each other and it was easier for them to show up for these auditions. They continue to conduct tests and leave their contact details to be contacted.

They're both auditioning for the movie « West Side Story ». A first audition is performed and they are then called back for a second audition which follows a first selection. This is for Stefanie her sixteenth dance hearing. She was summoned a few days later to a dialogue test on screen for the role of Velma.

She then turns to her mother to perform her rehearsals. His mother had met a family well known in the world of theatre in the « Yiddish » of New York, the Adler family, of which Stella Adler was known as a teacher and in particular for having as a student : Marlo Brando.

On the day of the test, she meets the actor who will give her the line: Rudy Solari. He later opened a drama school and Stefanie would have the opportunity to work on roles.

The on-screen test will be conducted with director Robert Wise. A beginner with no experience, Stefanie passed this first test and was summoned to present herself for other takes. All the dancers come from New York, except Stefanie Powers who is the only dancer from the West Coast.

But before she signs her contract, she must first obtain her work permit. As a minor, she must have a work permit and be accompanied by one of her parents. Integrated with the dancers recruited in New York, she begins her rehearsals. The studious atmosphere prevails in goldwyn Studios, which has set up a dance hall with a bar and mirrors for rehearsals under the leadership of Mr. Robbin, who will later become Natalie Wood's private secretary.

After rehearsals, the group of dancers listens to the recorded interviews between youth on New York's Lower West Side. According to Wise and Robins, they must create their own character and build their relationship in the band in order to understand and explain their opposition to the group of Puerto Ricans, which is the theme of the musical.

These first theatre classes will remain engraved in his

memory. The dance rehearsals were relentless and brutal. Robbin was demanding in the extreme, which revealed both his genius and his dark side. The remarks they address to the dancers are borderline humiliation and it demands the best of everyone.

Rehearsals follow each other for dance numbers before the main roles are perfectly defined.

The following days saw the arrival of Russ Tamblyn, Rita Moreno and George Chakiris, not to mention the arrival of Nathalie Wood accompanied by Robert Wagner.

Nathalie Wood and « RJ » (Robert John) Wagner were the dream couple of Hollywood youth. They were on the front page of every movie magazine. They were young and beautiful. They were all in awe of them. The rest of the cast attends rehearsals for these stars. It is a magical moment for everyone to rub shoulders with a generation of simple young actors who do not hesitate to spend time with them for their greatest happiness.

The studio organized its own press campaign to announce the roles of its main actors, including that of « Maria » to Natalie Wood.

Unfortunately, Stefanie Powers will have to give up rehearsals because of her young age (15 years) and her studies. She will be replaced by Carole d'Andrea who played in the role of Velma on Broadway. She will be heartbroken, but will remain in contact with Rita Hyde and Georges Chakiris as well as Harvey Evans.

She will also keep dating Tom Laughlin, who was about to launch his second film and was looking for a young girl for one of his roles.

To make his film, Tom had raised considerable funds from his hometown of Milwaukee (Wisconsin) where the film should be shot. He needed a young, innocent and inexperienced actress for the role of his high school and she fit perfectly with the character.

She was still working on « West Side Story » when the script supervisor, Bruce Kessler introduced him and his mother, a friend: Tom Laughlin. As her mother tells her : «When one door closes, another opens ». She began acting classes at 20th Century Fox, MGM and Columbia Pictures Studios. « Being able to meet throughout your life people you have worked with is a source of joy and also a guarantee of longevity », she said.

These studios were establishing contracts for their players and Stefanie Powers will sign her first seven-year contract, two films a year. The studios have a perfectly developed help to build future talented actors, be it courses in comedy, makeover, make-up, hairdressing, style, fashion and even a dentist. The wardrobe is developed by the studios that created a model for their actresses and actors.

Rules are established for rehearsal and filming days. Schedules include hours of work, arrival and departure for each day. Courtesy rules are a place where everyone is called by name.

Her first movie « <u>Tammy Tell me True</u> » July 26, 1961. Stefanie plays the role of « Kay », a young high school student in this American comedy/romance produced by Universal.

Before leaving for military service, her brother Jeff sold her his car, a 1958 Porche Carrera. Stefanie Powers loves sports cars and drives her Porch every day to the studios. It is when she arrives late to the Colombia, that she knocks out half with a swinging door, a man who wears the same sunglasses as her : Blake Edwards. It is a producer and its offices are located on the fourth floor. After her brief meeting with Blake Edwards, she was summoned for an interview. She auditions with her mom by her side with her partner, Lee Remick, who treats her like her little sister.

Chapter 2 : I'm an actress

Stefanie Powers begins filming of « Experiment in Terror » in 1962, it's a Black Edwards movie distributed by Columbia Pictures with Lee Remick and Glenn Ford.

A great complicity develops between Lee Remick and Stefanie Powers. This friendship will take hold over the years and they will both meet on the set of the series shot in France : « Mistral's Daughter » with Stacy Keach. « A psychotic killer, Garland « Red » Lynch, is waging a terror campaign with cashier Kelly Sherwood (Lee Remick) of San Francisco to force her to steal $100,000 from the bank for him. Despite her threats to kill her and her little sister (Stefanie Powers) if she goes to the police, she contacts the F.B.I. office in San Francisco, where Agent John Ripley (Glenn Ford) takes over the case ».

Glenn Ford plays the f.B.I. man, but appreciates his

character only a little. Stefanie Powers will shoot a single scene with him, near a swimming pool and during their presentation, he will ask her if she knows her text.

« Experiment in Terror » is a black polar with an excellent scenario. Blake Edwards innovates in a style of new Hitchcock-style techniques. Married to Julie Andrews, he remained very close to Stefanie throughout her life. William Holden, Stefanie Powers' companion, will be his wedding witness.

She played in 1962 « The Interns », a drama directed by David Swift and distributed by Colombia Pictures. This is the story of a group of newly appointed young interns arriving at the New York Hospital. Their lives, their daily struggle, their professional and sentimental trials. This low-budget film nevertheless made a great place at the Box Office and she will meet Cliff Roberson who will later play with William Holden in « Pique-Nique ».

Inger Stevens was a very beautiful actress whose life unfortunately ended with an accidental overdose of drugs. Nick Adams was a funny, wild man and a great friend of Natalie Wood and Robert Wagner. He was regularly seen in magazines alongside them. His life ended just as accidentally.

That same year, Columbia made the first loan of his

contract for a salary of $400 per week. She turns in « <u>If a Man Answers</u> » in 1962, it was a comedy directed by Henri Levin for Universal : « Chantal (Sandra Dee) is a young and seductive American whose success is such that she soon finds herself with three fiancés at once. Her mother (Micheline Presle) a sophisticated French woman and her father a rigid American businessman each want to put an end to this ridiculous situation and prepare her for a happy marriage. Arriving in New York with her parents, Chantal falls in love with an art photographer who took her as a model and before the injunctions of her father, the wife ».

In 1963, Columbia made a second loan for Warner Brothers. It will be « <u>Palm Springs Weekend</u> », a comedy that was a huge success with American youth because of its cast : Troy Donahue, Connie Stevens, Stefanie Powers, and Robert Conrad who will star in : «The Wild Wild West », and especially the famous « Pappy Boyington » of the series « Black Sheep Squadron » which will be a huge success : «In the seaside resort of Palm Springs, as at every Easter period, it is the invasion of students who take advantage of their fifteen days of vacation to come and get healthy under the California sun. Police forces fear this state of annual siege. As for their leader (Andrew Duggan), he will have to be vigilant this year now that his daughter, Bunny (Stefanie Powers) is old enough to flirt with this youth who thinks only of one thing, sex. This spring, 1963, a basketball team comes to mingle with the party. Jim (Troy Donahue) the captain, after having eyes during the bus trip only for the mysterious Gail (Connie Stevens), is going to be attracted to Bunny, while Gail falls under the spell of a rich arrogant playboy, Eric (Robert Conrad). Strech (Ty Hardin), a Texan stuntman, is not insensitive to Gail's blondeness while the troupe's joker, Biff (Jerry Van Dyke), will turn around Amanda (Zeme North), a tomboy judo champion. The passionate-lovers do not spare the older ones, the owner of the hotel where the basketball team went down to put the grapple on their coach (Jack Weston). Despite a good-child atmosphere, some will not come out unscathed...».

Connie Stevens and Troy Donahue were actors under contract with Warner Bros., which offered them some advantages, including personalized parking. As for Stefanie Powers, she has to state her name to the keeper every day and she is given a sticker in her name, which she must stick on her windshield. She brings her lunch every day.

She joins a team of girls from « Softball » who are all actresses and who come from New York, whose coach is simply a writer and producer on the rise: Aaron Spelling. He contacted him a few years later with Tom Mankiewicz and Robert Wagner, to propose the series: « Hart to Hart ».

Her first boyfriend is Peter Brown, he was working on one of Warner Bros.' iconic series. With her friends, Dean, Jeannie and Dino Martin, she plays tennis in their home on Mountain Drive. They are young and have fun. They are invited to parties with Danny Kaye, Sammy Cahn, Johnny Green and many others.

It was during one of their evenings that she met Bobby Kennedy and shared some dances with him. He is interested in what young people think and their involvement in American life. She had the opportunity to work for him during the 1968 presidential campaign. After this evening with Bob Kennedy, she will join Joan Collins and Warren Beatty to finish the evening.

Max Arnow sent her to Paramount Pictures for an interview with Batjac Productions. She is interested in Western films and « The Searchers » is her favorite movie. She loves westerns and John Wayne, but doesn't know that Batjac Productions is the production company created by John Wayne.

Her audition was successful and she got the role, with Carlo's Yvonne, Jerry Van Dyke, in the cast. The film is produced by Michael Wayne and directed by Andy Mc Laglen and Patrick Wayne.

Her second movie of 1963 will be « McLintock », a

western with John Wayne, Maureen O'Hara, George Washington « G.W. ». «McLintock (John Wayne), owner of the largest ranch in the area, has everything to be happy: he is rich, respected and feared by everyone except his pretty wife Katherine (Maureen O'Hara) who returns after a two-year absence, to file for divorce and get custody of their daughter Rebecca, « Becky » (Stefanie Powers). But neither of the two future ex-husbands intends to capitulate to the other. The tone is set and the low blows can begin ».

With an imposing budget ($2,000,000), this western is supervised by its star the Duke himself, who had from the beginning the idea of making it a shimmering family western and good child bringing together most of his relatives or faithful collaborators, whether in the cinema or among members of one's own family. Part of the filming was done in Arizona.

This twelve-week experience of filming was incredible. The Green Ranch was located in Nogales on a high plateau giving an extraordinary view of the magnificent landscapes.

It was in the fall of 1963, when she left the family home to go to the studios, that she heard the news that would shake the whole world : « President John Fitzgerald Kennedy had just been assassinated in Dallas », that will be in november 22, 1963. In front of the television, the first shocking images came from Dallas and the Parkland Hospital where President John

F. Kennedy had been transported. The country remained frozen, as did the whole world, mourning both man and history.

She headed for Burbank where a party scene was to be filmed. Balloons, confetti and paper coils seem frozen in time and space. The world was in turmoil and the rest of the decade will be stirred up with the escalation of violence, the Vietnam War, the Black Panthers, the riots of the Democratic Convention in Chicago, the riots in France at La Sorbonne, not to mention the Prague Spring, Woodstock, the assassinations of Martin Luther King and Bobby Kennedy.

On June 6, 1968, while finishing his speech at the Ambassador Hotel following his victory in the California primary, Robert Kennedy was shot in the head. It was when she left for the evening to which she was invited, that she attended in front of her television station the assassination of Bob Kennedy. With her husband Gary Lockwood, however, they went to the Ambassador Hotel to meet the rest of the guests to share their grief.

It is in the next few months that Stefanie Powers takes her independence by leaving the family home. Very close to his mother, they will have a fusional relationship throughout his life.

She travels to Mexico City to meet friends of the family

passionate about Corrida that she discovers. She is fascinated by the breeding and breeding of bulls and admires the vocation of matadors. The world of bullfighting perpetuates the translation of these ancient rites.

Back in Acapulco, she goes to the Hotel « El Présidente » where no room was reserved for him. The front desk finds a small room in which she crams her suitcases.

Then she receives a script entitled « Die ! Die ! My darling » filming will take place in England. She'll meet Tallulah Bankhead.

Filming takes place the following year in London : « An American woman, Patricia Carroll (Stefanie Powers) arrives in London to marry Alan Glentower (Kauffmann). She wants to see Mrs. Clover (Tallulah Bankhead) the mother of her fiancé Stephen who died in a car accident, who lives in an English village. She's a religious fanatic who resents Pat, and holds her captive. She will be released thanks to her fiance ».

Tallulah Bankhead is an American actress born in Alabama to a wealthy Southern family. Born into a dynasty of politicians and daughter of the governor of Alabama, she has a wild beauty and a stormy character. Her mother died at birth. From an early age, she betroed into theatre. At the age of fifteen, Tallulah Bankhead already performs regularly with local troops from her town. The following year, she won a beauty contest that opened up new horizons for her. Accompanied by her aunt, she sets out to conquer Broadway, but her bad temper will play her bad tricks. She refuses to shoot in John Barrymore's film, « Dr. Jekyll et Mr. Hyde » (1920) and moved to London in 1923. Thanks to the many plays she performed with her troupe, Tallulah Bankhead became famous and quickly became a star of Anglo-Saxon theatre. Her tumultuous private life and especially her bad manners earned him to be excluded from certain films. She decided to put her film career on hold to devote herself only to theatre. She returned to the cinema in many films and shot for Hitchcock « Life Boat » which will be her penultimate film.

Twenty years later, she arrived on the set of « Die ! Die ! My darling ». She moved to the Ritz and arrived in Limousine on the set supervised by young assistants, she was sixty-three years old. She died in New York in 1968 at the age of sixty-six.

In 1965, Stefanie Powers participated in the feature movie « Loves has many faces » for the Colombia : « Kitty Jordan (Lana Turner) a pretty billionaire is married to Peter (Cliff Robertson) a venal playboy. While on vacation in Acapulco, Peter discovers the body of his wife's lover. The police are leading the investigation. Around the wrist of the corpse, a bracelet on which is inscribed : « Love is a thin ice ». Carol Lambert the deceased's sister quickly arrives at the scene and becomes in love with Peter's main suspect. Then the girlfriend of the deceased (Stefanie) and Pete have an affair Carol Lambert the deceased's sister quickly arrives at the scene and becomes in love with Peter's main suspect. Then the girlfriend of the deceased (Stefanie) and Pete have an affair ».

In 1966, she shot the remake of « Stage Coatch » for 20th Century Fox, directed by Gordon Douglas. This film is the remake of 1939 movie directed by John Ford. The cast includes Ann Margret, Red Buttons, Mike Connors, Bing Crosby, Robert Cummings.

She joins the Wayne family and her mom is even integrated into some scenes. They toured Arizona with Indians from Utah. Filming will last twelve weeks on incredible sites such as The Green Ranch in Nogales. Located on a high plateau, with wide views of the sky and golden grasses, the Ranch is an essential location for filming. They travelled in a caravan on a winding road along a river to reach the endless meadows. The knowledge of local drivers is more than useful. To avoid breathing too much dust on their daily hikes, simply plug in the car's ventilation and shift the air intake controls to be recycled.

While Andy McLaglen is in pain and has to return to Los Angeles, it is John Ford himself who takes over. His arrival on the set was a very strong moment for the whole crew. When the taxi door opened and John Ford came down, dressed in a

Saharan woman, a scarf tied around the blow and a hat. This moment will remain engraved for everyone in their memory.

In 1967, it will be the film « Warning Shot ». A drama about a police sergeant killing a man during a safe house, and then he has to prove that it was self-defense. The cast includes: David Janssen, Ed Begley, Keenan Wynn, Sam Wanamaker, Lillian Gish, Eleanor Parker, George grizzard, George Sanders, Steve Allen, Carroll O'Connor, Joan Collins, Walter Pidgeon, Vito Scotti and David Garfield. The paths of many of these actors cross again with Stefanie Powers, including Steve Allen who will appear later in an episode of « Hart to Hart ». Joan Collins will also have an appearance in one of the Telefilms « Two Harts in three quart Time » (1995).

In 1985 the first installment of the TV mini-series « Hollywood Wiwes » is broadcast. It is a three-part adaptation of Jackie Collins' book about a group of very rich, attractive, snobbish women who are in Hollywood's lower life and high society. The miniseries has an incredible cast: Candice Bergen, Joanna Cassidy, Mary Crosby, Angie Dickinson, Steve Forrest, Anthony Hopkins, Roddy McDowell, Suzanne Somers, Robert Stack, Rod Steiger, Andrew Stevens and Catherine Mary Stewart.

At the age of twelve, Stefanie Powers received an

archaeology book as a Christmas present. Since then, she has dreamed of visiting the tombs of Egypt and walking on the Nile.

While filming the movie « Die ! Die ! My darling » ends, she reads in the press stories about the flood of the valley that could flood some of the precious temples of Upper Egypt. International teams of archaeologists were dispatched to locate certain buildings, such as the tomb of Ramesses II. She estimates the cost of the trip and decides to go to Egypt with her mother to visit the ruins of the Egyptian tombs. Her mother is equally involved in the preparations for the trip and consults all the guides on Egypt.

The journey begins with obtaining a visa that is slow to come. After a stay in Paris at the Hotel Georges V and once their visas are in their pocket, they land in Cairo where they are greeted by many press photographers in a crowd more than memorable. Mass tourism did not yet exist.

After visiting the National Museum, they visit the Valley of the Kings and the site of Karnak. They have the privilege of visiting the tomb of Queen Nefertari and making a crossing of the Nile aboard a sailboat called felucca, which is also used to transport cattle and goods.

They are given the opportunity to discover the quarries of pink granite where the manual work of the size of stones is always carried out as it was for the monuments at the time intended for the pharaohs. From their Old Cataract Hotel, they witness the construction of the Aswan Dam while enjoying the evening, a rosé gin from their veranda.

They both have wonderful memories of extraordinary landscapes on the Western territory from this trip.

Back in California, Stefanie began her search for a home in Beverly Hills and made her first acquisition for $42,000. A friend of his, actor and decorator, George Furth, throws a party to hang his housewarming. The house is on three levels and as she descends a flight of stairs, she meets her future husband, the actor, Gary Lockwood. The two of them had already met in a photo shoot for the magazine « Stars of Tomorrow » and he had starred in the film « Splendor in the Grass » with Natalie Wood and Warren Beatty.

Chapter 3 : Gary Lockwood

Gary Lockwood was born on February 21, 1937 (real name John Gary Yurosek) in Van Nuys, California, near Los Angeles. Actor, he began his career as a film stuntman, then in roles in « Warlock » in 1959. He also appeared as a policeman in Perry Meason in 1961.

In 1968, he was one of the stars of Stanley Kubrick's sci-fi film « 2001, A Space Odyssey » which will be a huge success. He will play with Stefanie Powers (his wife at the time) in the episode « Love American Style » 1969 and will participate in two episodes of the series « Hart to Hart » in 1979 and in 1983.

Between 1959 and 2004, he played roles in some forty theatrical performances and just as much on television. On August 27, 1966, he married Stefanie Powers, but the couple divorced on August 6, 1974. In 1982, he married Denise DuBarry, from whom he divorced in 1988 and had a daughter.

Gary Lokwood is not particularly appreciated in Stefanie Powers' family, especially by her mother who finds him a certain lack of education, but Stefanie Powers is attracted to Gary Lockwood. It was around this time that she met an actor known as Rock Hudson. Elegantly natural, he likes to entertain his friends, whom he receives on weekends for a music festival that includes Portia Nelson and Marion Wagner.

Marion Marshall will be Robert Wagner's second wife. After her marriage to Nathalie Wood in 1957, the two actors separated and divorced in 1962 following Natalie Wood's affair with actor Warren Beatty. Robert Wagner met Marion Marshall, a mother of two boys who lives in Rome. They married on July 21, 1963 and had a daughter together : Katie Wagner, born on May 11, 1964. The couple divorced in 1970, after ten years of living together. Robert Wagner and Natalie Wood married a second time on June 16, 1972. Together they had a daughter : Courtney, born on March 9, 1974 in Los Angeles.

The evenings at Rock Hudson are an opportunity to sing Broadway musicals. Peter Roche was a fashionable decorator in Los Angeles. He has decorated many houses of personalities including that of Robert Wagner. He will provide an important help to Stefanie Powers in decorating her home.

Leaving for London, Gary Lockwood presented him with the screenplay for « 2001 A Space Odyssey » which is almost virgin. Stanley Kubrick inventing the story of his film as he goes along. The spacecraft was built in the largest MGM studio in England and the spacecraft centrifuge wheel was built vertically. Outside, lights were bolted to the chassis.

MGM bought Stefanie Powers' contract from Colombia and in 1966 she made a television series entitled « <u>The Girl from UNCLE</u> ».The four-season series consisted of twenty-nine episodes aired on NBC. It was based on the character played by Stefanie Powers. Her character: Annie Dancer is a beautiful young spy in the service of the international organization U.N.C.L.E. Perilous missions lead him around the world and lead him to brave the danger. Its beginnings of gadgets, will pave the way.

On August 27, 1966, Stefanie Powers married Gary Locklood in Hollywood in the presence of their family. Stefanie's mother will not attend the ceremony and so will Gary's parents. They set off on a yacht with their friends to Catalina Island.

The couple's separation took place eight years later. She

puts her stuff in her car and goes home to her mom. On the same day, Roddy Mc Dowall invited her to a party, and she met Ava Garner and Elizabeth Taylor in difficult conditions, to whom she tearfully announced her divorce.

Thus began his friendship with the two women. She will reunite with Ava Gardner, who will play her sister, on the set of « Mistral's Daughter » during an episode shot in London, it will be one of his last appearances. The divorce of Stefanie Powers and Gary Lockwood was finally pronounced on August 6, 1974.

In 1974, she starred in a western « Gone with the West », with James Caan, Aldo Ray, Robert Walker Jr. A film that she will describe as mediocre because of its scenario. The interior scenes are filmed in a studio that belonged to American International Pictures near downtown Los Angeles. Real prostitutes play their own role in the film. Filming continues in Las Vegas, where the team is housed at the Mint Hotel. After a sandstorm overnight, the exterior décor is heavily damaged.

She travels to Buenos Aires with Fernando Lamas with whom she has toured « The Girl from U.N.C.L.E. ». Buenos Aires is one of the most beautiful cities in South America. The men are elegant and remarkably dressed. After a week of festivities, she goes to Bolivia. Two thousand feet above the sea, the capital La Paz is the highest city in the world. With a serious headache due to altitude, she consumes on the recommendation of the Hotel, tea called coca mate. People chew coca all day long, which they use as a sedative.

Few tourists at that time were travelling to the Andes. It takes the bus towards Lake Titicaca, then the train to Machu Picchu. She befriends a student on the bus to Lake Titicaca. The road leading to Macchu Picchu is narrow and the ruins emerge from the mist.

In the twentieth century, steamboats arriving from England brought their passengers to the lake leading to Bolivia. The journey will continue on a small steam train to cuzco. Locals tend to travellers spit-cooked corn cobs and coca mate. The market square of the city is the shopping paradise from which it will return with a poncho in colorful tones, woven with Lama wool. She will spend the night in a hotel/youth hostel, they will be awakened in the early morning by Lamas who have come to beg for a few crumbs of bread.

Enjoying the liners, she will have the opportunity to make several crossings to France on board one of these luxury boats. Her interest in travel began in Mexico, where she learned the language and culture. Then came the discovery of Japan and Europe. These trips, which are organized as part of the promotion of films, are also an opportunity for excursions. Moreover, one of her trips to Europe took her to Rome.

In 1962, she went to Rome with her mother to promote her film « Interns ». At a ceremony held at the Vatican, people are honoured and awarded a medal for performing acts of kindness. Among them, Marcello Azzena and his wife who own a small house on the outskirts of Rome. Despite their limited financial means, they are home to abandoned and mostly abused children. They care for twenty-seven children who live under their roofs, from the age of three to sixteen. The living conditions are very simple, and they do not have hot water.

Together with Maude Muller of Colombia, they make bags containing shoes, sweaters, sweets, toys for each child, as well as a large basket of food, which they load into their cars. They go to the site followed by an army of journalists and photographers. All the children are waiting for their visit. The house is clean and simple. Mattresses on the floor are the children's dormitories. The children are proud to welcome them and display their best smile.

For Sefanie Powers, her eyes stop at a little boy just nine years old: Silvano. Taking affection for this little man who was not insensitive to the young woman, Stefanie and her mother come together in order to be able to help this family.

After collecting donations and making his own contribution, work is carried out in the house, in order to bring all its occupants more comfort. Hot water is installed, as is a washing machine, as well as food aid.

Stefanie Powers and her mother go to the Embassy to find out the formalities for adopting little Silvano. Unfortunately, because of her age, 21 years old and not married, he could not adopt the boy. Nevertheless, she maintains a close relationship with the child, whom she sees every year, and also helps this whole family.

After her marriage to Gary, she thought she could adopt the child, who was now thirteen. But her husband objected, for he did not accept the young boy. She will remember it bitterly and will continue to contribute to her education.

In 1979, he obtained a visa as a student to travel to the United States. Stefanie Powers lives with William Holden in Palm Spring, who takes care of the young man while she divides her time, between Beverly Hills and Palm Spring, on the series « Hart to Hart ». Through Tom Mankiewicz, producer on the series « Hart to Hart », William Holden proposes to Silvano to work for one of his friends, Cubby and Don Brocoli on small gardening jobs.

In the evening, the young man makes fresh pasta to the delight of the Broccoli couple. Silvano meets Barbara, the daughter of the Broccoli couple and speculates to marry her because he finds her very pretty and this would allow him to obtain U.S. citizenship.... But Don Broccoli suggests that it would be more prudent to remain an Italian citizen... rather than becoming a dead American citizen....

Some time later, he had to return to Italy, his visa being completed. Later, he had his small business with his wife and three children.

In 1970, she starred in an episode of the series « It takes a Thief » alongside Robert Wagner. The series consists of thirteen episodes. This series tells the adventures of a thief hired by the American Secret Service to act as a spy. Al Mundy is a high society player.

The original title « It Takes a Thief » is the abbreviation of a proverb : « It Takes a Thief to Catch a Thief » (It takes a thief to catch a thief), and there are obvious allusions to Alfred Hitchcock's film « To Catch a Thief » as well as the vogue of secret agents that has swept the world in film and television since the triumph of the James Bond « Goldfinger » in 1964.

In 1970, she starred in the series « Medical Center », with James Daly and Chad Everett. The daily life of surgeons faced with tensions between the younger generation of doctors and elders.

In 1972, Stefanie Powers appeared as a Guest Star in the television series « The Sixth Sense », in the episode entitled « Echo of a distant scream ». «When she returns to her old home, Ruth Ames (Jane Wyman) begins to see visions, including that of her long-dead daughter, Mindy. Her other daughter, Jean (Stefanie) did not believe her at first, but things are changing.. With Gary Collins, Dennis Dugan, Gene Evans, Mike Lane and Rod McCary in the cast.

Gary Collins had already teamed up with Stefanie in the TV series, « Love American Style » the previous year, and Gene Evans would later be seen in one of the episodes of « Hart to Hart » in 1981.

In 1972, she starred in the film « The Magnificent Seven Ride ».

« A lot of things will be different after this movie », she said. « It was hell, we found ourselves without stuntmen for women and there were men missing to play cowboys and Indians. So what have we done? I put on a wig and Became an Indian ».

In 1972 and 1975, she was a partner of Michael Douglas in episodes of the series « The streets of San Francisco ».

In 1973, Stefanie Powers appeared in an episode of the television series « Medical Center ». In this episode, titled « Fatal Memory », she plays the role of Aggie a free aviator, haunted by the accidental deaths of her husband and child, who becomes suicidal.

In 1974, the TV movie « <u>The Golden Cage</u> » is broadcast. She plays the role of a beautiful socialite accused of murdering her husband. He was actually the pilot of the TV series « Petrocelli ». A large cast that includes Barry Newman, Susan Howard, Jon Cypher, Henry, and Ralph Meeker, and Dennis Patrick.

The same year the TV movie « <u>Skyway to Death</u> ». In this thriller the life of a passenger car hangs in a delicate balance when an aerial tram is paralyzed in a windstorm.

In 1974, it will be the film for television « <u>Shoot out in one dog town</u> ». The story of a banker who is forced to protect his city from a vicious gang of bank robbers determined to get the $200,000 stored in his bank . It includes Richard Crenna.

In 1974, Stefanie Powers appeared in the episode of the series « <u>The rookies</u> ». It is an investigation into the death of a newlywed police officer, who is hampered when his widow, who is also a police office, seeks revenge. Also in the world is James Woods.

« <u>Herbie Rides Again</u> » sort en 1974. A real estate agent, Alonzo Hawk, wants to build the largest building in San Francisco but his project is not successful because Mrs Steinmetz, owner of a former barracks, refuses to leave the premises. Tired of harassing her, Alonzo changes tactics and sends his nephew, Willoughby, a naïve and gentle young man, to meet him. But he clashed violently with Mrs. Steinmetz's allies: the ravishing Nicole (Sefanie Powers), a tram and the Volkswagen car.

She appeared in 1976, in an episode of the TV series « Bionic Woman », partner edits Lindsay Wagner and Lee Majors.

In 1977, she appeared in the episode « Affair of the Heart » of the tv series « McMillan ». Among the actors, she finds Rock Hudson and Larry Hagman.

In 1979, she was alongside Roger Moore in « Escape to Athena » a British film, starring David Niven Telly Savalas and Claudia Cardinale : « In the Greek islands in 1944, men worked in a German prison camp, under the direction of Professor Blake (David Niven), a captive archaeologist, to exhume important archaeological pieces. Supposed to be sent to Germany, the most beautiful are actually sold on the black market by Commander Hecht (Roger Moore), camp leader ».

Chapiter 4 : William Holden, the meeting

After her divorce, she had to look for a new home. His various investments in real estate projects during his marriage to Gary Lockwood are frozen pending the judgment of their divorce. Her Malibu land is the subject of a new coastal planning commission imposed by a California law. Unable to continue the work or resell her land, she must resolve to find other solutions.

Having completed her studies before the bachelor's degree and as a resident in California, she is determined to make up for this time and immerses herself in the knowledge she lacks in various fields including financial management..

She obtains a list of books required by UCLA University and spends her next two years filling those months of study by reading the two hundred books as mentioned on the list. To this end, she is trained as a financial manager in order to better control her assets and expenses.

Since 1970, many tennis tournaments have been organized by celebrities for charity. These events raise funds and redistribute them to charity. One of these tournaments will change his life. She also met Charlton Heston, Clint Eastwood, Abby Dalton and Debbie Irwin.

In 1973, one of his high school friends, Doug Grant, wanted to rent his house near Benedict Canyon. These are small cottages close to one another. The atmosphere is like a village, with neighbours, artists, musicians, composers and actors. It was the perfect place for Stefanie Powers.

Her first meeting with William Holden occurred on a New Year's Eve party with friends, Lennie and Dominick Dunne. The evening takes place in the company of Moss Mabry, a costume designer. This one, gone to get drinks, Stefanie Powers finds herself face to face with William Holden, who introduces himself. This first contact was extremely brief and consisted of wishing himself a good year, but he left her under his spell.

It was while shopping at a bookstore on Santa Monica Boulevard in Beverly Hills that she discovered several photographic books devoted to Africa. Immersed in the reading and discovery of these books, she startled when someone leaned over her shoulder : « Take this one », he told her. Turning around, she finds herself confronted by William Holden who asks her if she is interested in Africa. To this, she replies that she knows only Egypt. «Well, he said, if however, you go to Kenya, don't forget to come and see me». Before he could even realize and be able to answer him, he had already disappeared.

They meet again at the seaside resort of La Costa where she is invited by Merv Adelson, partner at Lorimar Productions, who produces a miniseries with William Holden and Lee Remick. Their next meeting will be at the tennis tournament, followed by a cocktail where William Holden will invite Stefanie Powers to dinner. They'll meet in a small restaurant. Following this dinner, he will invite her the following weekend to his residence in Palm Springs. Having already had a lunch with her family, Stefanie will have to decline the invitation.

His aunt Helena and uncle own a house in this part of the desert. She and her mom drive at night to get to Palm Springs. She leaves the family party to join William Holden.

William Holden is a travel enthusiast, his Palm Spring home is full of memories of the Far East and his passion for Africa. He has a great concern for art and his collection represents his whole life. He has a curiosity about the world. It began on her first trips to Korea, Japan, Singapore, Hong Kong and Africa in the 1950s. Japan is recovering from the war and Korea is in the middle of a conflict. He meets new, exciting and influential people.

On a trip from Jakarta to Singapore, his flight was in turmoil. The passengers were violently shaken. A man sitting right behind him handed him a vial that they both shared during the journey, his name was Johnson. Johnson was number two at the U.S. Embassy in Singapore, which meant he was also a member of the C.I.A.

On this Sunday, both arriving by the morning flight, he invites her for the evening to a barbecue. From this new circle, William Holden will meet two exceptional people, Malcolm Mac Donald who was helping in the transition from countries that became independent following the colonies and one woman : Han Suyin.

Of Eurasian origin, she has just finished writing a book about her life, and her love affair with an American journalist, whom she met in Hong Kong and was killed on a mission. He will devour the reading of this book entitled : «The most beautiful things » and will contact Paramount to purchase the rights to the book.

The film will be produced with Audrey Hepburn and William Holden as the main actors. This will be the trigger for its attraction to Hong Kong.

In 1974, William Holden joined the film crew « The Towering Inferno » with Paul Newman, Steve McQueen, Faye Dunaway, Robert Wagner, Richard Chamberlain and Fred Astaire : «In San Francisco, the world's tallest skyscraper will be inaugurated with many guests including promoter Jim Duncan (William Holden), his public relations manager Dan Bigelow (Robert Wagner). Its architect, Douglas Roberts (Paul Newman), sees this evening turn to drama when a short circuit causes a fire and blocks the guests on the 135th floor of the building. Michael O'Hallorhan (Steve McQueen), the city's fire captain, is responsible for commanding the rescue operation..».

When William Holden started the film, Stefanie Powers was in Austin, Texas, where she starred in a play. Her mom wants to accompany her to Texas and suggests driving his Chevrolet Blazer, which Stefanie Powers bought a few years ago.

Having just left California and arriving in Arizona, the air conditioning suddenly stops. They decide to drive at night to benefit from better road conditions. In a road restaurant, a truck driver suggests they follow a truck closely to benefit from the suction.

She receives an invitation to play tennis for a charity in Hong Kong. William Holden and Stefanie Powers wait until the end of filming to go together. After landing at the old Kai Tak airport, they return to their hotel, « The Mandarin » , located on the colonial side in Hong Kong, aboard a Rolls Royce that sent them to the hotel.

The Hong Kong of 1972 is a long way from present-day Hong Kong and still has colonial-era buildings. We can differentiate between different cultures and social strata. The sounds and smells of Hong Kong are a sensual overload of emotions. From the moist air, to the unspoiled softness of starched white cotton, it's a range of exotic pleasures that envelops you in splendour.

The tennis tournament will take place ten days later.

Quite elegantly, William Holden has booked two rooms at the Mandarin, located next to each other. She meets him the next morning for breakfast, and they will spend the day with friends in Kowloon before returning to Hong Kong by ferry in the evening. They exchange their first kiss on the Ferry back to Hong Kong.

After a week of romance, William Holden had to travel to Bangkok and then Kenya. After that first night, Stefanie is so in love that she will write the only poem of her life to her knowledge, which she will give to him to read it on her return journey, while she will stay a few more days in Hong Kong.

William Holden (Born Franklin Beedle Jr.) is an American actor born on April 17, 1918 in Illinois. He was one of Hollywood's biggest stars in the 1950s and 1960s, alternating starring roles in classic films, including « Snset Boulevard », « Stalag 17 », « Sabrina », « The Bridge of the River Kwaï », « The Bridges at Toko-Ri » ou « The Wild Bunch ».

He toured with the biggest stars of the time including: John Wayne, Alec Guinness, Humphrey Bogart, Peter Sellers, Gloria Swanson, Audrey Hepburn, Grace Kelly, Deborah Kerr and Barbara Stanwyck.

A seductive with striking beauty and athletic physique, he was an emblematic actor of this heyday in Hollywood. It is ranked by the American Film Institute (AFI) 25th Legend Star.

William Holden's parents had moved to South Pasadena. His father was an industrial chemist and suffered from heart problems. Her mother was a schoolteacher. William Holden was already an adventurer at heart. He was having fun walking the length of a bridge over his hands using the gates. This bridge was later dubbed the « The bridge of suicide » due to the large number of suicides caused by the Great Depression.

William Holden was the eldest of three children and was

the son of a schoolteacher, Mary Blanche, and an industrial chemist, William Franklin Holden. The family moved to California when he was three years old. Coming from a middle-class background, nothing predestined him to a career as an actor.

A graduate of South Pasadena School, he entered South Pasadena High School to continue his scientific studies. He discovered radio and theatre and played in many plays at the amateur level.

He moved to New York with a friend, dropping out of school to follow in the same footsteps as his father, and made his Broadway debut with Bob Ben Ali in Manya. At twenty, he plays a character who is sixty more. He was then spotted by Milton Lewis, a talent hunter with the powerful Paramount Pictures, who offered him a six-month contract.

One Sunday, during a meeting between William Holden and the manager of his kansas hotel suite, the hotel was not air-conditioned and his bedroom windows were open. William Holden argued that he could perform a stunt that consisted of running to catch a freight train.

In order to prove to his manager that he could perform this stunt, he jumped out of his bedroom window from the top of the fifth floor and found himself hanging out, standing on the window sill. The director was convinced and yielded at the request of William Holden.

Having never belonged to a gymnasium, however, he had a natural athletic and physical ability that remained so throughout his life. Pasadena, California had the seat of the Pasadena Playhouse. Built in 1925 with the first world works of F. Scott Fitzgerald and had in his school of actors, Raymond Burr, Charles Bronson and Dustin Hoffman, it was a place of discovery of talent for Hollywood studios.

William Holden participated in his first play at the Lycée and auditioned at the Passadena Playhouse. His mother is not very enthusiastic, but he will be able to continue as long as his academic results are satisfactory.

His father, despite his health problems, lived to the age of seventy-six and witnessed the success of his eldest son. His younger brother became a pilot during World War II, where he tragically died in the South Pacific. As for his second brother, he will take over the family business. His mother died in the 1990s.

After a small role in « Three Faces East », he got a leading role alongside Barbara Stanwyck in « Golden Boy ». His role as a violinist turned boxer points to him. He played roles in minor productions of Paramount Pictures and Columbia Pictures, and became William Holden. During World War II, he served as a Lieutenant in the Air Force and met Brenda Marshall, who had a one-year-old daughter from Virginia whom he married in 1941. They had two children:

Peter and Scott.

Soon after, Pearl Harbor, William Holden enlisted in the army. Upon his return to civilian life, the film industry changed. There are many players competing for the same jobs, and he is moving towards radio soap operas, plays and commercials. He is slowly rebuilding his career. When Ronald Reagan was elected to the Actors Guild Screen, William Holden became its vice-president, and he became the godfather of their daughter Patti.

He returns to success thanks to Billy Wilder who hires him for the legendary « Sunset Boulevard ». His role as an unlucky screenwriter earned him an Oscar nomination for Best Actor. The film is now considered among the greatest films in the history of cinema.

He behaved as a popular star the following year in « Born Yesterday » with Judy Holliday. Two years later, with his new fame, he toured « Stalag 17 » of the same director. This time it's the consecration and he gets the Oscar for Best Actor. Its popularity is growing, especially among women. He is elected « Most Popular Male Star of the Year » at « Photoplays Award » in 1954 and 1955.

William Holden moved with his family to Switzerland. This allows him to give his children an international education and a substantial financial advantage, due to the tax in

Switzerland.

In 1952, he shot the film « The Bridge of the River Kwai » and will receive a $1 million stamp. He bought a penthouse apartment in Hong Kong, on Robinson Road in a building designed by one of his friends, Al Alvarez.

The previous year, he went to Africa with two friends, a Swiss banker and an American industrialist, for a hunting safari. They'll buy a hotel. In 1960, the hotel named « Mount Kenya Safari Club » reopens its doors, and it will become the destination in East Africa. Kenya is about to become independent and is attracting the world of Jet-Set.

In 1966, he acquired two thousand hectares around the Safari Club. Together with his friend, Don Hunt, he created a Ranch for The Preservation of Species, which would be one of the first in East Africa.

He filming in « Executive Suite » Robert Wise in 1954, where he met Barbara Stanwyck. Along with the rest of the cast, he won the special jury prize at the Venice Film Festival in Italy. The filming of « Sabrina » is more difficult: he can't stand Humphrey Bogart and falls in love with Audrey Hepburn.

His reputation as a man to women did not fade with his subsequent roles. He rubbed shoulders with Grace Kelly twice in « The Country Girl » and « The Bridges of Toko-Ri » , Kim

Novak in « Picnic » in 1955 and Sophia Loren in « The Key ». William Holden continues to shine in manly productions that only contribute to his international success. He plays in « The Bridges of the River Kwaï » of David Lean in 1957, whose success was such that he assured him enough money for the rest of his life, and he was a physician opposed to John Wayne in « The Horse Soldiers » de John Ford.

In 1964, he reunited with Audrey Hepburn « Paris When it Sizzles ». He will say : «I realized that I was going to have to see Audrey again and take control of my alcohol problem. However, I did not feel able to face either of these situations ». The affair he had — then married — with Capucine, a former and elegant French model, did not help matters. He often gets drunk on set, and even has to stop shooting for a few days.

In 1967, he toured « Casino Royal » and returned to the war film the following year for « The Devil's Brigade » de Andrew V. McLaglen . Mais, c'est surtout le film de Sam Peckinpah, « The Wild Bunch » which seems to be the culmination of this second career. From then on, he slowed down his career. He did, however, play several important roles in the 1970s, alongside Bourvil in « The Christmas Tree », in « Breezy » by Clint Eastwood and in the famous disaster film « The Towering Inferno »,1974, alongside Paul Newman, Steve McQueen and Robert Wagner.

In 1976, he shared the poster for « Network » Sydney Lumet with Faye Dunaway. A critical film on the evolution of television, and then that of « Fedora » by Billy Wilder with Marthe Keller (1978). These are his last big roles. He also played with Paul Newman in 1980, in « When Time Ran out ». His last movie is « S.O.B » by Blake Edwards alongside a number of stars, including Julie Andrews.

A long-known alcoholic, William Holden has never been able to overcome his problem and will have a tragic end.

According to the Los Angeles County Medical Examiner's report, William Holden was alone and drunk in his Santa Monica apartment. On November 12, 1981, he fell and opened his forehead severely on the ledge of his bedside table, bleeding to death. Evidence suggests that he remained conscious at least an hour and a half after his fall. It is likely that he did not realize the severity of his injury and did not ask for help, or was unable to do so.

His body was found on November 16, 1981, four days after his death. His remains are cremated and his ashes scattered in the Pacific Ocean.

A few months later, Barbara Stanwyck paid tribute to him, receiving her Honorary Oscar by declaring : « I loved him very much and I miss him. He always wanted me to have this Oscar. So tonight, my Golden Boy, your wish comes true».

A few years after her death, Stefanie Powers was asked to represent William Holden at the christening of two refurbished dubbing theatres at Sony Pictures. Both theatres were named in honour of William Holden and Kim Novak.

Back from Hong Kong, Stefanie Powers travels to Toronto to shoot a film. William Holden joins her for a weekend. It's December, after a few days together, they plan to spend les fêtes de fin d'années ensemble, à Palm Springs.

The return flight from Toronto makes a stopover in Chicago before landing in Palm Springs. The sun has been there and she can't wait to find William Holden. He is not there to welcome him. She leaves the airport alone and finds him in great discussion with police officers, standing near her Mercedes-Benz. He is clearly not fit to drive.

Stefanie Powers gets behind the wheel and they go home together. When he gets home, he goes straight to his room, to bed alone. She'll meet him in the early evening in the middle of a convulsion in his room. Paramedics will take him to the hospital. He will then return home, the seizures being due to too much alcohol.

She met William Holden's sons and their mother at the hospital. The meeting is cold. One of them will tell him «that it will not prevent him from drinking, all those who have tried, have failed ».

Stefanie Powers' uncle Howard tries to dissuade her from continuing her relationship with William Holden. But if, however, she wishes to continue living with him, she will have to learn to live with her alcoholism. As a former alcoholic, he has nearly touched a drink for more than thirty years, but he is still an alcoholic.

They were at the beginning of their relationship and it was not an easy situation for Stefanie Powers. Confronted brutally with William Holden's alcoholic problems, she is aware of the problem and wishes to stay with William Holden, as she herself will say, she has the character of a Polish woman and wants to learn to live with the one she loves.

William Holden was an icon in the world of cinema, like others, no longer part of this world, he was a true living legend. Many women had fallen in love with him because of his charm and attraction to women.

While William Holden is recovering at the Hospital, she makes the decision to help him as best she can. His discussions with his uncle are present in his mind, and the meetings he attended at Alcoholics Anonymous allowed him to remain sober.

She returned to Toronto for forty-eight hours to finish her film and moved back to her cottage in Yoakum Valley. William Holden loves this part of the California desert, as do other actors, such as Robert Wagner and Natalie Wood, who settled there after their second marriage and bought a house near Palm Springs.

William Holden loved to ride his motorcycle and they would go on long outings on the weekend. On the slope of Southridge was the place where William Holden wanted to build their house. He seemed to control his alcohol consumption and was limited to a few beers. William Holden owns an apartment in the desert, and it is there that he takes refuge, to drink with a friend, Frank Shappe who was his commercial director.

Back in Los Angeles, Stefanie Powers couldn't reach William Holden on the phone. She learns from her housekeeper that he is definitely in her apartment in Palm Springs.

Needing help, she enlisted the help of William Holden's lawyer, Deane Johnson, who also owned shares in the Ranch in Kenya. They end up with a friend of William Holden, Marty, who advises her to contact Alcoholics Anonymous. They both knew William Holden and witnessed his addiction to alcohol, but were convinced that William Holden's love for

Stefanie Powers might perhaps help him overcome his illness.

All three of them headed to Palm Springs to expose the situation to William Holden. This was the best thing for William Holden, who was persuaded to attend the Alcoholics Anonymous meetings.

These meetings brought him what no clinic, which he had known elsewhere in Europe, had brought him. He is enthusiastic and will attend a seminar with Stefanie Powers. He was beginning to open his mind to other ways of thinking.

For the next five years, William Holden managed to maintain his sobriety, which allowed them to live the five best years of their lives together.

Together, they discover the world and it lives through the eyes of Stefanie Powers. This transmission of knowledge that he would have liked to communicate to his children, he will do it with her who wanted to learn everything about him and his passions.

They have the same passion for travel, Stefanie Powers having already discovered many countries before her meeting with William Holden, just as they enjoy walking around Death Valley or on the Colorado River. But she had to know her baptism of fire in the form of an initiation into William Holden's other life : Kenya.

In 1958, while moving to Switzerland, William Holden reunited with two of his friends : Ray Ryan and Carl Hirschmann for his first safari in Kenya.

Ray Ryan is the owner of the El Mirador Hotel in Palm Springs, as well as a Casino in the Caribbean. Carl Hirschmann is a banker in Switzerland in Zurich, where his family founded the Bank of Credit, Handels.

This is not the best time to travel to Kenya, due to independence and guerrilla fighters, the Mau Mau who camp in the forests in the country. The atmosphere is tense and the population is armed. After arriving in Nairobi, they equip themselves with weapons for their own safety. Tourism is not yet relevant, and it will develop from thc 1970s on.

This safari requires many preparations, and the commitment of a professional hunter. The hunting areas have been organized into small blocks, and are consistent with the management of wildlife services. Hunters are allowed to draw a specific quota.

Such a safari requires significant financial costs. As they change their camp, they arrive at a house called « The Mawingu ». It is a house built on the slopes of Mount Kenya, with a magnificent view of the glacier covered with peaks of ice open on the equator. Rhoda Lewinsohn and Gabriel Prudhomme are a couple who decided to settle in Nanyuki, Kenya where they built a house.

During the Second World War, Rodha Lewinsohn had to return to the United States, and her husband Gabriel Prudhomme, as a Frenchman, joined the fighters in Algeria.

The house will be sold to a family who owned two hotels in Nairobi. Later, in light of the events of the 1950s and the insecurity, the « Mawingu » will go on sale.

After buying the « Mawingu », William Holden goes on safari. He purchased two thousand acres of land surrounding the Safari Club to create a Ranch for wildlife and culture preservation. It will become «The Mount Kenya Ranch Game ».

Chapter 5 : William Holden, The Kenya

In 1974, Stefanie Powers went to Kenya with William Holden. This is her first trip to Africa. They arrive in Nairobi and are greeted by their friends, Don Hunt and Iris Bridenben. Don Hunt, is a red-haired man and is an Irish Catholic from Michigan. As for Iris Brideben, she is blonde and of German descent. After making purchases, they take the heavily loaded road in their Land Rover towards Mount Kenya.

After twenty-two hours of flying and at more than 7000 feet of altitude, it is good to be able to rest. Their room located in a small cottage has a shower, and is part of a line of cottages rented. From the site, we can see the second highest mount of the African continent : The Mount Kenya.

The « club » called the Mount Kenya Safari Club, lives up to its reputation. The place seems to have an exceptional attraction for lovers of grandiose landscapes. It also offers special services for their guests, allowing them to leave the business and equipment used for the safari.

William Holden introduced her and his friends to capture zebras, which had to be moved south of the country to protect them from poachers. She falls in love with Kenya as much as the man she loves : William Holden.

They share the same passion for domestic and wild animals and their environmental curiosities. Mount Kenya Ranch captures live animals in East Africa. Some of them are sent to zoos and zoos around the world.

Their camp is established in the northern border where the Grevy's zebra is about to disappear. This is to transport them to a national park located in the south called Tsavo. The Grevy's zebra is a species only found in Kenya. Large in size, it has thin stripes and large ears.

Each day starts at dawn with tea and cookies, then loaded vehicles are loaded ready to go for shipping. The Jeep used is basically a military vehicle that has been modified a little according to the needs of the expedition, and must allow the capture of the animals safely.

The captured animal receives an injection of vitamins, as well as an antibiotic to reduce intestinal parasites that could multiply as a result of the stress of capture. No animals are slaughtered unless they have been injured.

Stefanie Powers is in one of the Jeeps with Iris Bridenben. She takes countless photos and will finish the expedition by helping with injections.

The zebras are gathered in a paddock, surrounded by a bamboo mat, to protect the animals from sight. They receive food, cut grass and water. They continue their journey and go to Lake Rodolphe or Lake Turkana and meet the El Molo Tribe.

William Holden knows them well and already organizes a regular shipment of cornmeal to supplement their fish-based diet. They reach the town of Lamu on the coast, which was once a port for traders.

The Arab influence is dominated by architecture, the way of life, and the call to prayer at the Mosque. The city is populated by craftsmen who make furniture and wooden doors. They will leave with two carved wooden chests and a door. It will take them a year to get to California.

They land on the island of Zanzibar. At the time, the rules for allowing access to the country were different and they did not have a permit. The overgrowth pilot is in shorts and not in a suit, which is not acceptable to Muslims, and doesn't help matters. They get permission to stay for one night at the only hotel in the area, their pilot being dressed with a stito on their legs. The shops are closed and the place looks like a ghost town with the exception of their hotel.

They continue their journey and leave the next day for the crater of Ngorongoro. They spent three days in Addis Ababa and met william Holden's friends there. Having accepted an invitation to the Jury of the Film Festival in Tehran, they make a stopover in Athens. The city is under the snow just like Tehran. Alex Smith and Craig Stevens, two friends of William Holden, are also present at the Festival.

Their guests are part of the royal family, and it is the Minister of Culture, who has been married to one of the Shah's sisters, who is the organizer of the Festival. Stefanie Powers meets Empress Farah Palhavi. She accompanies him on the organized tour of the Crown Jewels in the centre of the city.

Returning to the Hilton Hotel is difficult due to traffic at this time of day. They returned to Switzerland and walked along Lake Geneva before returning to California and Los Angeles.

While William Holden was on a trip to New York, Stefanie Powers joined him and handed him a letter from Papua New Guinea. President Sumari offering them to take care of the sale and promotion of art in Papua New Guinea.

The President wants to create artisanal industries in order to develop the artisanal economy which represents the traditional way of life of the majority of the population.

Knowing William Holden's interest in local art, he offered them the exclusive right to represent the Art of Papua New Guinea for the whole world. The idea came to them to create a department store to group the works of art and market them.

For his part, President Sumari organizes cultural centers so that works emanate from villages can be deposited there. The National Museum suggests creating a seal of authenticity for works.

Their arrival at the first cultural centre in Sepic was a disappointment. Despite the building, no organization, no representative of cultural affairs being present. They are taken to different villages to negotiate the purchase of a few coins.

It is the women who are the intermediaries for the sale. They follow their husbands' instructions and negotiate prices with buyers. They meet Ebia Olewale, who is a member of the Government. He comes from the Gogodala tribe who are renowned for their tribal art.

The sculptures produced use the same primary colours used by the artist Alexander Calder. All purchased parts are numbered and photographed before being shipped.

For their return trip, they make a stop in Bangkok before returning to Munich where William Holden is to make a son about the events on the tragic Olympic Games in Munich. In the Thai capital, they meet william Holden's friends. Descended to the Oriental Hotel, they enjoy the hotel's well-being and shop for silk clothes, while recovering from those days in the bush.

Stefanie Powers returns to New York where their two partners are waiting for her. Together, they carry out an inventory of the 465 pieces they bought in Papua New Guinea. Part of it was sent to Los Angeles and will be exhibited in a West Hollywood Gallery, run by friends Gail and Chuck Feigarten. Their company W.A. Stefrick Imports Ltd had just been launched. William Holden's many trips to Hong Kong also have an attraction to China. Nixon's visit to China in 1972 unlocked the early stages of trade.

In 1977, they went to Beijing (Bejiing). The country retains the scars of the last earthquake that killed 250,000 people and lives in the post-Mao era. Obtaining their visas being subject to spending 50,000 dollars of items emanating from their guests.

Their first visit to a china warehouse outside Beijing was a real disappointment. The patina was dull and a large number of porcelains had cracks. As for Jade's plays, they were poor quality reproductions.

The next day, on a Sunday, they visit the Great Wall of China. Most of the people they meet wear a uniform. Mao-style jacket and pants are made in two colours: grey or navy blue. No Western clothing is available for purchase. They pass through the Tiananmen Gate, the main entrance to the Forbidden City.

Back at the hotel, Stefanie Powers is attacked by a man with a knife. Her partner, Richard, throws himself at the assailant, he will be wounded in the shoulder and taken to the hospital. William Holden arrives with their friend, Ani followed by a group of police men and journalists.

The press became agitated with the arrival of William Holden and it was only later that they learned that officials had been warned that W.A. Stefrick Imports Ltd was owned by a famous American actor and a television actress working on a series in Hong Kong.

News of the incident went around the world in less than twelve hours. A full report of the incident landed in Washington. One of the persons who intervened to transport Richard by taxi to the hospital was an American working for Kelloggs in China.

The incident has an immediate effect on the pursuit of the wanted objects. They are suddenly offered quality goods reserved for long-standing customers, such as carpets, antique porcelain. They attend a dinner hosted by the Mayor of Beijing and the Head of the Revolutionary Committee.

Stefanie Powers made many trips to China, and bought a house in Hong Kong that had belonged to William Holden.

Back in Los Angeles, Stefanie Powers undergoes tests that reveal she has contracted hepatitis. She stays in bed for five weeks.

His agent then offered him a film with David Niven, Telly Salavas, Roger Moore and Claudia Cardinale, which would be shot in Greece, on the island of Rhodes, and which has the title « Escape to Athena » (1979).

Stefanie Powers and William Holden travel to London to produce the film. It is a British film, directed by Georges Cosmatos, set during the Second World War, when prisoners working on archaeological sites try to escape.

In 1978, Stefanie Powers was contacted to play the role of Roxane in « Cyrano of Bergerac ». The play was to be performed in San Francisco and then in New York. As rehearsals began, she was contacted by Tom Mankiewicz, Robert Wagner and Aaron Spelling for a new television series called « Hart to Hart ».

Tom Mankiewicz is a long-time friend and has been successful as a screenwriter and has just rewritten the pilot of the series that was originally called « Switch double ». She has known Aaron Spelling since her marriage to actress Carolyn Jones. As for Robert Wagner, we have to go back to the days of « West Side Story » when she met him and Natalie Wood. She had also performed alongside him in the series « It takes a Thief ».

When « RJ » saw Tom Mankiewicz's script, he wishes to have for his « wife » in the series, Stefanie Powers with whom he had got along very well on a previous shoot, and thought that the alchemy would be perfect. For its part, the production wants to impose on him the actress Lindsay Wagner for the duo « Wagner/Wagner » facing the duo of the series « Hart to Hart ». Robert Wagner informs the production that there will be no series, if the role is not assigned to Stefanie Powers.

The first of « Cyrano of Bergerac » gets good reviews. William Holden joins her backstage with roses in hand. Her mother was present at this premiere and the production moved to San Francisco. A union strike begins and will last nearly three months.

Stefanie Powers joins the filming of the pilot of the series « Hart to Hart » which takes place in the « Quinta Resort » located not far from William Holden's house in Palm Springs. The other actors, Roddy McDonwall, Stella Stevens and Jill St John (who will be Robert Wagner's third wife in the city) get along just fine. Natalie Wood (who was Robert Wagner's wife at the time) also appeared in the pilot. The script is well written which facilitates the work of the actors. The chemistry between Robert Wagner and Stefanie Powers is perfect.

Until the production agrees to air the pilot's episode and the series can continue, Stefanie Powers and William Holden leave for Kenya. One of their associates, Ray Ryan, who owned a stake in Mount Kenya Safari Club, is under tax control in the United States. Carl Hirschmann, the third largest shareholder, also wants to sell his interest in the case. William Holden has no choice but to sell his shares. The entire Club was sold to entrepreneur Adnan Khashoggi.

Shortly thereafter, Ray Ryan was murdered on his way out of his club in Illinois when his car exploded. Iris and Don Hunt, who lived on the Ranch, had built a guesthouse that they wished to keep at the disposal of William Holden.

The sale of the estate comes at a time when the film industry is changing. This is a difficult time for William Holden, who isolates himself and occasionally consumes alcohol.

Stefanie Powers resumes filming of the sequel to the series « Hart to Hart ».

One of his tenants in Benedict Canyon leaves one of his houses he occupied. His small family grows with Senor, a wonderful feline, Papuga a yellow amazon who will be his companion for thirty-seven years and a German shepherd. Her mother takes care of her animals during her absences, whether on sets or during her travels, and she is her main support in her relationship with William Holden.

William Holden's alcohol problems resurfaced. In

particular, during periods of depression, which she describes as « a female lover » so demanding, that nothing can hinder it. It was unfortunately in these alcoholic episodes that William Holden twice asked her to marry him.

Her mother moved into a house she had built on one of her properties, her building being demolished. William Holden enjoys Stefanie Powers' family, but he is a loner and needs his moments of isolation, and he moves into an apartment he owns in Santa Monica.

A few days later, the production asked him to pick up William Holden. It was a Friday, she drove him home. A friend on the casting offers to make him meet a doctor at a Clinic specializing in addiction, where he will stay on the weekend. At the end of the shoot, he joined the Clinic again. She joins him for an interview with the Doctor and William Holden sets it happy. The doctor asked him not to see William Holden again during some necessity for his care.

The series « Hart to Hart » spends all his time. The first season is demanding and the days are long. « RJ », Robert Wagner is quite charming, but he is also a caring friend. The same is true of Lionel Stander and Tom Mankiewicz, who looks after his actors. He is also a perfectionist director, and everyone recognizes his talent.

The whole team is a real family. The series works which

allows the production to make episodes in prestigious locations such as the station of Vail in Colorado.

After weeks of silence, William Holden and Stefanie Powers reconnect. William Holden receives the film script « The Earthling » in 1980, with Ricky Schroder and Jack Thompson. Filming is to take place in the Australian outback. Although he still attends Alcoholics Anonymous meetings, he made the decision to move to Australia. The whole team stays in mobile homes and William Holden enjoys filming.

Filming was over and before returning to Los Angeles, William Holden went to Hong Kong and stayed in a hotel run by a friend. Stefanie Powers loses phone contact with him, which leaves him considering the worst, when it comes to a new alcohol consumption. He finally returns to his apartment in Santa Monica.

After a few days, he contacted Stefanie Powers. He is expected to join the team « SOB » (1981) by Blake Edwards, with Julie Andrews, Marissa Berenson. Stefanie Powers goes on set, and the atmosphere is very nice like all Blake Edwards productions. She joins him after a day's work in his apartment in Santa Monica, but finds that unfortunately, she can only make the observation, that he still consumed alcohol. At each of his alcohol attacks, he feels the need to isolate himself which allows him to recover until the next alcohol crisis.

They celebrate the new year 1981 together. William Holden goes to Kenya to make a documentary for NBC. His stay continues and their friends, Don Hunt informs him that William Holden drinks heavily.

Leaving Don Hunt's advice to join the Clinic in California, he goes straight to his apartment in Santa Monica. He phoned Stefanie Powers the following weekend to inform her that he wanted them to build a house in the Ranch part of Kenya and wanted to start a youth education program for wildlife conservation.

.

At the end of the first season of the series « Hart to Hart », Stefanie Powers goes to China, then to Hong Kong before returning to Los Angeles, the last week of July. William Holden picks her up at the airport and they go to the home of friends who own a house on the beach : Billy and Audrey Wilder for a BBQ.

In the fall of 1981, the filming of one of the episodes of the series « Hart to Hart » takes place in Hawaii. She no longer receives phone calls from William Holden. She leaves him messages, but he doesn't call her back.

On her return to Los Angeles, the filming takes place on the pier in Santa Monica, it's a Friday. She is about to spend the weekend in one of her houses in Malibu that she has just finished renovating. She stops in front of William Holden's building and rings, but gets no answer. She keeps calling him on the phone, but to no avail.

On Monday morning, she goes back on the road and goes on the set while listening to the news on the radio, when she hears those words that tetanizes her: « veteran actor William Holden ….». Time remains suspended.

She returned home and contacted William Holden's lawyer. His masseur, Chet, had gone to his home and William Holden was intoxicated. He would later have fallen because of a carpet in his room, his head having hit the corner of his nightstand. The deep cut severed the artery, which would have resulted in death for the next 20 minutes, according to the coroner.

The shock is immense for Stefanie Powers and her friends join her in her house, Robert Wagner and Natalie Wood being the first to show up. She receives countless phone calls, flowers. Iris and Don Hunt will take the first plane to join her. The next two weeks are a summary of emotions, between loss, death, remorse, anger, abandonment and love.

William Holden's family organized the funeral without any consultation with Stefanie Powers. The actor's body will be cremated. It was a second shock for Stefanie Powers, who came out shocked and wounded and unable to implement The Wishes of William Holden.

She organizes a meeting of friends at her home, which

will give rise to many testimonials from her friends.

The following week sees the Thanksgiving celebration. With the support of « RJ », Robert Wagner, she goes on the set of the series « Hart to Hart ».

At the end of this second season, Stefanie Powers returns to Africa. Following the reading of William Holden's will and after long discussions with Don and Iris Hunt, they decided to create a memorial for William Holden. The William Holden Wildlife Foundation was born, inspired by William Holden's idea to build a wildlife conservation training center.

Back in the United States, Stefanie Powers set up a public charity to raise funds.

Due to his success in the series "For the Love of Risk", doors opened and allowed him to use his notoriety in the service of the Foundation. Knowing business leaders, lawyers, these contacts allowed him to create partnerships. A first major instalment was made by Gordon Mc Lendon, who owned a radio and television station in Texas, at a dinner party and presented her with a check for $10,000. The next day, at the scene of the filming, Robert Wagner presented her with a check for $10,000. Fundraising and in general the activity of women of wealthy celebrities. The world of Polo will open the doors for him to organize charity competitions. She will form a team with Stacy Keach, Pamela the wife of Manuel Rojas, who was an excellent Polo player.

More than 40 people will join them, including Sammy Davis Jr, Lorne Greene, Budy Hackett, the entire team of the series « Hart to Hart » don't forget the dog Freeway. A buffet was organized for 1500 people and 150,000 dollars were raised. In the years to come, the team included William Devane, Steward Copeland, Geoffroy Lewis, Tommy Lee Jones, Sylvester Stallone, Mohammed Ali, Joanne and Paul Newman.

When they went to Kenya in 1982, they began working on architecture for the Education Centre. To date, more than 500,000 people have been welcomed at the Education Centre. The fight for the preservation of species never ceases. Despite the ban on the killing of endangered species, new forms of poaching are emerging. Rhinoceros horns have been smuggled out of Africa in diplomatic suitcases for the new rich in the Third World.

Chapter 6 : William Holden,
The Mount Kenya Safari

In 1974, Kenya was Stefanie Powers' first trip to East Africa with William Holden. Together with his financial partners and friends, Don and Iris Hunt, he introduces her to Kenya. Their interests and passions are mutual. The only thing she does not share with him is her addiction to alcohol. An addiction that he was able to keep at a distance more or less during their nine years of life together, but from which he will not win the last part.

Now Stefanie Powers is alone to take the dusty roads that lead to the Laikipia Plains. So many landscapes that are so familiar to her. How could he imagine a few years earlier that from his meeting with William Holden would leave him such a legacy of East Africa, of Kenya.

Her old Toyota Land Cruiser accompanies her on these

roads, at the mercy of a breakdown or a puncture. This trip is different from the others, so different. She calls every night in California to hear from her mother, who is in good health, and gives her details of her days.

She's got to stay strong. She must be strong to recover from her lung operation, following the discovery of her cancer. She must remain positive to overcome the disease. And how not to continue?

In the mid-1950s, William Holden travelled to Africa to take part in a hunting safari with two friends. The word Safari, meaning « travel », it was for many years associated with a journey of « hunting ».It was synonymous with elephant hunting, away, leopard and buffalo. William Holden and his friends stay edit in Kenya for several weeks despite unrest in the country. The hostel they are staying in is for sale, and they do not hesitate to buy it back. It will become : « The Mount Kenya Safari Club ».

Located on Ecuador at 7000 feet above sea level on the slopes of Mount Kenya, it overlooks gardens and forests as far as the eye can see. The hostel undergoes many transformations to make it the most beautiful hotel in East Africa.

It is important to remember that conservation, preservation and even the concept of ecology were ideas that would not become popular vernacular until several years after the creation of the Mount Kenya game ranch. Green movements in the United States and the United Kingdom have raised awareness of wildlife conservation through T-shirts bearing the face of a baby seal that has come to our streets and lives.

William Holden and his friends were pioneers in animal conservation and created the « Mount Kenya Game Ranch » in which they set up game breeding programmes and dozens of East African species (including endangered antelopes) as well as an orphanage. Throughout his life, William Holden continued his support for his reserve. In 1973, he introduced his partner, Stefanie Powers, to discover Africa, his passion.

After her death, Stefanie Powers created the « William Holden Wildlife Foundation » to carry out his unfinished business and pursue his dream. The Foundation has been a recognized public charity since 1982.

The William Holden Wildlife Foundation :

Spread over beautiful, well-designed lawns on the slopes of Mount Kenya with cranes and peacocks crowned in grey, the Fairmont Mount Kenya Safari Club offers the ultimate Safari retreat experience that combines relaxation and leisure with living spaces comfortable, exemplary, discreet service and sumptuous cuisine. A colonial-style property covering an area of 100 acres. Founded by William Holden, the Lodge has had a long list of illustrious visitors to join their Hall of Fame.

The William Holden Wildlife Foundation Educational Centre offers visiting students a unique opportunity to experience the outdoors in rare communication with nature in an exceptional environment. The preservation of flora and fauna is essential for the transmission of knowledge to future generations. Respect and teaching make it possible to exploit the resources available to man while preserving the environment.

The education of children who visit the Foundation through their school, allows them to communicate around them on the themes implemented, including model gardens used for projects that serve as an example to be implemented in their school, in the culture of vegetables and trees. Awareness of the richness of the environment, crops, plantations, composting. It is essential to continue research on animal production in captive breeding.

Captive breeding is an essential axis for the conservation of species and to maintain the population and preserve it from extinction. Although it is different, all techniques are being implemented to improve its development for species survival.

There are currently more than 500,000 animals in captivity in zoos around the world. At European level, there are about 2,500 species, which allows the reproduction of animals to be organised via a network set up in zoos.

Kenyan schoolchildren's first encounter with wildlife

The majority of Kenyan children do not have the opportunity to see the wealth of wildlife that their country has to offer. They can live in remote cities or rural areas. Most of them would not normally have access to the rich areas of the game. There are of course no zoos and a trip to the playground is out of reach for most families.

Several years ago, William Holden and his Hunt friends began inviting local schools to visit the animal orphanage of their Mount Kenya game ranch. The kids had a wonderful time. From there our educational programs grew.

Later, they founded the « William Holden Wildlife Foundation » to continue educational programs in memory of William Holden. The Foundation, chaired by Stefanie Powers, has become the first wildlife education center in Kenya that students can visit in the region.

The highlight of course remains a visit to the conservation and orphanage. Here, children can « touch and feel » all species of native fauna. Interns are part of the foundation which makes it easier for them to study. Others come during their holidays.

This center inspires schoolchildren (aged 11 and over)

from all over Kenya, regardless of their context, to think about conservation. A unique educational experience is conducted in the great outdoors, supplemented by interviews and films in the impressive library/conference theater.

The groups alternate activities at the center with a visit to the nearby animal orphanage. The program includes discussions around a campfire, quiz, treasure hunts around the nature trail, a weather station and activities such as planting trees, cleaning litter or dismantling traps. Older children climb a hill, study vegetation areas and the uses of native plants. They benefit from the center's outreach programs, and learn valuable lessons to lead to adulthood.

Recycling and conservation

Nature is designed to work in harmony. In a wetland that recycles all the sewage from the camp, the waste water is transferred to another pond that has been cleaned by plants and filtered through the stones. Manure is used to produce biogas and is used for cooking.

Learning to build by forming an ecological briquette made from sawdust, grass and leaf. A solar boiler provides water. A kettle is suspended and tilted to capture the sun's rays and thus provides hot water.

Groups of children plant trees and harvest seeds for the nursery, then bring the seedlings back to school. The estate includes ponds, ducks, geese, rabbits and vegetable gardens.

Stefanie Powers

Stefanie Powers is the mainstay of the William Holden Wildlife Foundation. She is the sublime wife of Robert Wagner in the series « Hart to Hart ». Her nine years of life with William Holden have anchored him permanently in Kenya. A year after her death in 1981, Stefanie Powers opened the center, fulfilling William Holden's dream.

William Holden's love for Kenya began on his first visit in 1964. His encounter with a big game hunter, Don Hunt, was decisive. Realizing the urgent need to protect Africa's animals, they bought land and founded the Mount Kenya game ranch in 1967, the first in Kenya. The ranch provided a safe haven for animals preserved as well as poachers, while animals were exported to zoos in the United States but also to other African reserves.

The Mount Kenya Wildlife Conservation

In 2004, the Game Ranch became the Mount Kenya Wildlife Conservatory. It has 1200 acres and includes 1,500 animals, or more than 28 species. This area is reserved for the breeding and rehabilitation of wild animals. Many animals are rescued such as white zebras, pygmy hippos. This centre provides care and allows them to be released into the wild. The orphanage collects baby rhinos, cubs, elephants, cheetahs or chimpanzees.

Some animals, such as monkeys, are then released into family groups. Rubshoulders, baboons, cheetahs, monkeys, bush pig.

The Bongos

Bongos are Central African antelopes. They are herbivorous mammals that belong to the bovid family. The African antelope is the most colorful on the continent, and it is becoming increasingly rare in the wild. It has long horns. The bongo is recognizable thanks to its red brown colour striped with thin and vertical white lines. The main threats to bongo are poaching, and the gradual destruction of its habitat. In some areas, it also faces total elimination.

In the 1970s, studies indicated a drastic decline in Bongo's populations. About 20 animals have been transferred to zoos in the United States to breed. Then, a first group was reintegrated into Kenya in 2004. It is one of the most successful conservation projects in the world. There are currently more than eighty bongos in the forest of Mount Kenya.

At the heart of the project is the animal orphanage, a private and funded facility, unique in East Africa, for the care and rehabilitation of young, abandoned, sick or otherwise vulnerable animals and their eventual return to nature.

The development

William Holden was involved in numerous animal capture operations. Slowly, the ranch fills with animals, and after breeding, they will return to their original habitat. As poaching increases, the center welcomes a large number of orphans.

The process of rehabilitation and liberation is never simple, but it is also the constant goal of the ranch and its orphanage. African students are invited to participate in these conservation programs. The entire foundation and its operation are funded by donations. It is one of the world's recognized conservation organizations. Mount Kenya has been recognized by the United Nations as a World Heritage Site.

Chapter 7 : Hart to Hart

In 1978, Stefanie Powers was contacted to play Roxane in « Cyrano of Bergerac ». Filming was planned in San Francisco and then in New York. At the beginning of rehearsals, she was contacted by Tom Mankiewicz, Robert Wagner and Aaron Spelling. They are about to make a pilot for a new TV series called « Hart to Hart ». Tom Mankiewiecz is a long-time friend. She had met Robert Wagner and Natalie Wood during rehearsals on « West Side Story ».

This series « Hart to Hart » was originally to be played by Lindsay Wagner in order to form the on-screen duo « Wagner/Wagner ». But that's without counting on Robert Wagner who does not want another actress to play his wife in the series that Stefanie Powers. But that's without counting on Robert Wagner who does not want another actress to play his wife in the series that Stefanie Powers. They had played together in a series and wanted to continue this adventure. After a meeting with the Wagners, it turned out that their complicity would allow them to do this series.

The pilot of the series « Hart to Hart » started in Palm Spring in the « Quinta Resort » a few miles from William Holden's house in Palm Springs. This episode included the participation of Roddy McDowall, Stella Stevens and Jill St John, mutual friends, not to mention Natalie Wood who was making an appearance on the pilot. From day one, Tom Mankiewicz created a relaxed work atmosphere and a joyful atmosphere.

The story was well designed and the script well written, making the job easier. Moreover, the chemistry between Robert Wagner and Stefanie Powers was perfect, even if the first scene filmed was the introduction of Stefanie Powers through the window in Robert Wagner's bungalow, that she had to undress and slip into the bed near Robert Wagner and kiss him ... under the eyes of his wife, Natalie Wood who was on the set with their four-year-old daughter : Courtney.

It took several months for production to be completed and for the pilot film to be shown so that it could obtain approval for a series.

During this wait, William Holden and Stefanie Powers left for Kenya. The other two shareholders of the Kenya Club found themselves in a fiscal position that led them to part ways with the Club and William Holden was reluctantly to sell his shares as well. Don and Iris, who lived on the ranch, had built a guesthouse that they kept available to their guests.

Back in the United States, a sense of isolation has taken over William Holden, who again resumes occasional drinking. Although the Game Ranch and Wildlife Conservation was the realization of a project of which he was proud, his profession as an actor was his only source of income.

During the filming of the Pilot episode of « Hart to Hart », Stefanie Powers picks up one of her homes in Benedict Canyon that was rented, she settles there with her animals. His adopted son, Silvano, will join him there on his tourist visa.

William Holden is still confronted with his alcohol problems and is always looking for the comfort of his depressions in alcohol. Stefanie Powers' mother is her main support, especially to take care of the menagerie when she is on a trip. She will make an extension to her house to house her mother following the demolition of the building in which she lived.

Although he enjoys his family, William Holden is a great loner and prefers to move into his apartment in Santa Monica. He leaves for Hawai on a casting with Paul Newman and Jacqueline Bisset.

Upon his return to Los Angeles, the studios contacted Stefanie Powers to bring William Holden back. After lunch, he consumed alcohol and no longer fits on his legs. It was a Friday and the start of a long weekend. After much discussion, he agreed to join a clinic at St John's Hospital, which specializes in addiction. A week later, Stefanie Powers received a phone call from William Holden, who was enthusiastic.

She goes to the clinic to see him. He is in great shape and is much better. The doctor takes her aside and asks her why she lives with an alcoholic. Surprised by this somewhat brutal question, she is caught off guard.

They must separate for a time, the time of the possible healing of William Holden.

Hart to Hart - Pilot : «A friend of the Harts has a fatal accident on a highway leaving a sanatorium. The reasons for this death remain unclear, so Jonathan and Jennifer decide to investigate under a false identity and discover the particular methods of fitness of this institute ».

The series is part of investigations by Jonathan and Jennifer Hart, the billionaire vigilantes. true « Self-made-man », Jonathan has built himself through hard work, bold bets and willpower, a beautiful empire « Hart Industries ». Married to a former journalist, the businessman spends happy days in their cozy Californian nest. Regularly involved in cases of theft, smuggling, murder or even espionage, the couple improvise detectives to solve investigations that the police do not always want to explore.

The Harts are helped by their trusty butler-driver: Max, inseparable from their beloved dog, « Freeway ».

Filming of the series « Hart to Hart » is overwhelming and brings Stefanie Powers the professional joys that are shunning her personal life. The days are long and the filming is demanding, even if the first season is not a resounding success. Robert Wagner is charming, funny and is a caring protective friend. Together with Lionel Stander, they are all an incomparable team.

The series works and finds its audience, which allows them to hope for a second season. An episode is made in the prestigious ski resort of Vail in Colorado.

After a period of separation due to the detoxification of William Holden, they remain close and continue to see each other. He lives in his Apartment in Santa Monica and participates in a film that takes him away from the United States. When he returned, things changed again and it is obvious that he put an end to his abstinence.

The first season of « Hart to Hart – 1979 / 1980 » includes seventeen episodes :

1. Hit Jennifer : « Jonathan Hart, owner of the Hart shipping company, mingles with the dockworkers who work for him and discovers the underside of a national scandal....».

    2. Passport to Murder : « Jonathan and Jennifer Hart spend a peaceful holiday aboard their yacht in a small Mexican port.....».

    3. Jonathan Hart Jr : « One evening, Jennifer and Jonathan Hart receive an unexpected visitor: an 8-year-old boy who introduces himself as Jonathan Hart Jr. and with a letter from his mother Connie entrusting the boy to his father..... ».

    4. Dealth in the Slow Lane : « Jonathan Hart buys a beautiful and shiny old car from the turn of the century to give to his wife Jennifer. But, it turns out that the

Un destin : Stefanie Powers

machine is full of finds that makes it an outsized contraption….».

5. <u>You Made Me Kill You</u> : « One of Hart Industries' new secretaries is completely obsessed with Jonathan Hart and kills everyone who would make him give up the billionaire's heart…..».

6. <u>Murder Between Friends</u> : « A couple of friends of the Harts who are in the process of divorce is suspected in the murder of a famous lawyer….».

7. <u>Cop Out</u> : « Red-haired prostitutes are murdered in Los Angeles. Jennifer Hart, who knows the industry well for writing articles, decides to lead the investigation despite her husband's warning….».

8. <u>Max in Love</u> : « Max fell in love with a mysterious woman, Charlotte Fleming. But several small clues make the Hart couple unconfident….».

9. <u>A New Kind of High</u> : «Hart Industries Science Director Dies in Lab Explosion…..».

10. <u>With this gun I thee wed</u> : « The Harts receive an invitation to a wedding taking place on the French Riviera. But it would seem that the marriage was arranged under duress by a certain Alex Constantine, old enemy of Jonathan Hart…..».

11. <u>The Man With the Jade Eyes</u> : « A man fatally collapses at the Harts' table while they are dining in the Chinatown of Los Angeles. But before he dies, he

entrusts the billionaires with a golden statuette with jade eyes that they must take back to a temple...».

12. <u>Color Jennifer Dead</u> : « Warren Keller a painter friend of Hart is found dead after a car accident.....».

13. <u>A Question of Innocence</u> : « Rose, the newspaper saleswoman at the bottom of the Hart Industries building, is under the control of a blackmailer who asks her for money in exchange for her silence......».

14. <u>Night Horrors</u> : « The Harts are invited to a treasure hunt in the old mansion bought by Fred and Amanda from the couple's acquaintances. But very quickly, the evening slips with the death of one of the guests....».

15. <u>Which Way Freeman</u> : « Freeway has a new fiancée, the neighbor's. When the latter is murdered, Freeway takes the murder weapon and disappears with it. But back at Villa des Hart, he no longer has it with him....».

16. <u>Downhill to Death</u> : « Jennifer Hart is witnessing a discussion about planning a murder of a woman. This woman is the wife of Hasley Matthews and a friend of the Harts. But during a ski ride, it is not the wife who dies but the husband....».

17. <u>The Raid</u> : « When a Hart Industries technician is abducted in South America and a large ransom is

demanded, Jonathan and Jennifer Hart go there to make the transaction….».

18. <u>Sixth Sense</u> : « Sara Morgan, a young woman with extraordinary psychic abilities, has visions of her impending death. Jonathan and Jennifer Hart attend a session during a visit to the Hart Industries Parapsychological Section…..».

19. <u>Does She or Doesn't She</u> ? : « Politician's wife dies in car crash after discovering that information she held about her husband was made public following her affair with hairdresser Barry Saxon….».

20. <u>Cruise at Your Own Risk</u> : « A Cruise Line owned by the Harts is the target of a diamond thief who, on his last flight, killed a crew member. The Harts infiltrate passengers under a false identity to unmask the thief…..».

21. <u>Too Many Are Murder</u> : « A great cook has created a revolutionary recipe, but before he gives his recipe to the Harts, he is murdered….».

22. <u>Death Set</u> : « A woman accidentally kills her husband as a result of false allegations. The Harts who were close to the husband are trying to find out what happened….».

The second season of the series « <u>Hart to Hart – 1980 / 1981</u> » consists of twenty episodes :

1. <u>Murder On The Wall</u> : « Jennifer and Jonathan Hart meet an old acquaintance of Jennifer former model Marcie Fowler in New York….».

2. <u>What Murder</u> ? : « Jonathan Hart is to be reunited with a former friend at his downtown Los Angeles office, Drew Kendall. While waiting for him, he observes by the monocle of his friend the murder of a woman that takes place in an apartment opposite. He decides to rescue the young woman and runs but is hit violently by a biker. He's unconscious. When he woke up, he became amnesiac….».

3. <u>This Lady is Murder</u> : « Jennifer and Jonathan Hart are cycling when Jennifer is abducted by two men, Mick and Barney Steele…..».

4. <u>Murder is Man's Best Friend</u> : « While walking around the park with Freeway, Max is stopped by advertisers looking for a new dog for Dr. Cobb's pie….».

5. <u>Tis the Season To Be Murered</u> : « In one of Hart Industries' toy branches, plans for revolutionary new toys are stolen…..».

6. <u>Murder Wrap</u> : « Professor Whitlock was murdered while working on the new wing of the Los Angeles Museum on Egyptology. Jennifer who was one of her alumni helped create this new attraction with financial support from Hart Industries….».

8. <u>Ex-Wives Can Be Murder</u> : « Pearl Danko, Max's

ex-wife, is back in Los Angeles and wants to see him again. Jennifer and Jonathan Hart pick her up at the bus station and are attacked by two men who were trying to steal her suitcase….».

9. <u>Murder is a Drag</u> : « Jonathan and Jennifer Hart go to the opera when Jonathan realizes that he has forgotten the tickets at home. He buys two from a pickpocket who previously stole these tickets from a criminal charged with recruiting a killer to murder the attorney general….».

10. <u>Hart Shaped Murder</u> : « The Harts, in spite of themselves, witness the malfeasance of a group of diamond traffickers who use confectionery as a screen for their criminal activities….».

11. <u>Slow Boat to Murder</u> : « Stanley, Hart Industry's accountant, is the first suspect in a murder case. The body of a businessman was found on a boat with Stanley's papers nearby….».

12. <u>Murder in the Saddle</u> : « The Harts took their weekend to get to their ranch in New Mexico. But as soon as they arrived, their friend Tom Raintree was found dead near poisoned cows and buffaloes near a stream….».

13. <u>Homemade Murder</u> : « Millie, a new Hart Industry employee hid an old bullet in a jar in the Harts' living room….».

14. <u>Solid Gold Murder</u> : « Vince Nucona, Max's protégé, is going to open a weight room. While present, the Harts witness the attempted theft of Vince's dumbbells….».

15. <u>Getting Aweigh with Murder</u> : « The Harts infiltrate Hart's cruise line where counterfeit money seems to be smuggling….».

16. <u>The Murder of Jonathan Hart</u> : « After two failed murder attempts on him, Jonathan Hart organizes his fake murder with the complicity of his wife Jennifer, in order to find out who is behind this case….».

17. <u>The Latest in High Fashion</u> : « Jonathan and Jennifer Hart are invited to a Fashion Party where we find the body of a murdered supermodel. Suspicions are focused on Alexei Briansky who will also be killed in bizarre circumstances…..».

18. <u>Operation Murder</u> : « Jennifer Hart was hospitalized after an accident in the park. During the night, she witnessed the murder of a patient in a nearby room but fell unconscious….».

19. <u>Murder Takes a Bow</u> : « A playwright entrusts the new script for a play to Jennifer and Jonathan Hart. Soon after, he is murdered while part of an amateur troupe of a play where play our two heroes….».

20. <u>Blue Chip Murder</u> : « The Harts find a new room in their house by accident. During their

investigation, they are asked to report their discovery to the real estate agency responsible for the sale of....».

The third season of the series « Hart to Hart – 1981 / 1982 » includes twenty-four episodes :

1. Harts and Flowers : « Max created a rose he named « Jennifer Hart » and enters a flower contest. But Jennifer Hart becomes the target of a psychopath....».

2. A Couple of Harts : « On holiday in Acapulco, the Harts have a car problem that leads them to knock on the door of a rich villa....».

3. Hartland Express : « Air traffic controllers strike forces Harts to take train from Chicago to Los Angeles....».

4. What Becomes a Murder Most ? : « Jennifer Hart participates in an advertising campaign for a faux fur coat....».

5. Murder Up Their Sleeve : « A magician plans to replace Jonathan Hart at the head of his company with his brother whose face has been transformed by surgery....».

6. Harts Under Glass : « Jennifer Hart is kidnapped by a wealthy eccentric known for her many collections and who holds the young woman in a glass cage....».

7. Rhinestone Harts : « Country music star Lorene Tyler's international tour is produced by Jonathan Hart.

Her husband Jesse, a jewel thief, hid many jewels in Lorene's stage costume….».

8. <u>Hart of Darkness</u> : « A psychopath who blames Jonathan Hart puts a dangerous product in the pool. Jonathan Hart then burns his eyes to the point of going blind….».

9. <u>Hartbreak Kid</u> : « Monty, the trainer of the Hart horse at the horse race, is found dead in the booze-soaked box. Her adopted daughter Riley doesn't believe it all the more because she heard two men fighting with him….».

10. <u>From the Depths of My Hart</u> : « Off the coast of Hawaii, the Harts are experimenting with a new type of underwater camera near the wreck of a ship. Swimmer supposed to try it is found drowned with broken camera….».

11. <u>Hartless Hobby</u> : « The Harts visit the gallery of a famous philatelist to admire the Vermillion, the most expensive stamp in the world. When it ends up in their possession, their lives seem dangerously threatened….».

12. <u>My Hart Belongs to Daddy</u> : « The Harts join Jennifer's father in Washington. He is the target of a mysterious German who wants to avenge the death of his father….».

13. <u>Hart of Diamonds</u> : « After her appointment at the hairdresser, Jennifer Hart starts stealing jewelry

without realizing it. Her husband, Jonathan Hart discovers that the salon owner hypnotizes her clients to turn them into kleptomaniacs and thus recover precious objects…..».

14. <u>Harts and Palms</u> : « While in Hawaii, the Harts meet an old business friend of Jonathan's. Surprising a conversation, Jennifer thinks his wife plans to murder him. But it is finally his wife who finds death in a strange accident….».

15. <u>The Hart of the Matter</u> : « Jonathan and Jennifer Hart travel to France at the invitation of an old friend, who has given them an appointment in a mansion transformed into a hotel…».

16. <u>Blue and Broken-Harted</u> : « Jonathan and Jennifer Hart fake a public argument to make it look like their couple is in crisis and unmask whoever wants to cause their breakup….».

17. <u>Harts on Their Toes</u> : « The Harts come to the aid of a Russian dancer in love with an American woman and accused of a crime he did not commit….».

18. <u>Deep in the Hart of Dixieland</u> : « For one evening, Jonathan Hart re-forms a jazz band with old friends. But during the evening, the wife of one of them is found murdered and the friend in question is immediately arrested….».

19. <u>Vintage Harts</u> : « Jonathan Hart's partner in a

wine company discovers that their win e« Hart-Cabri »
is marketed in bottles of a much more expensive
Château St Claire vintage. But the man is soon murdered
and the Harts will have to investigate to discover the
deception…..».

20. Hart, Line and Sinker : « Eager to rest in their
mountain cottage, Jonathan and Jennifer Hart must help
their young guard accused of murder by the sheriff. But
it is the latter is in fact the perpetrator of the crime….».

21. Hart and Sole : « Back from the dry cleaners,
Jonathan's jacket was exchanged with another. Wishing
to return it to its owner, the Harts went to the hotel
where he stayed. But in the room, they find only a
corpse….».

22. The Harts Strike Out : « A collaborator of
Jonathan Hart suddenly dies leaving behind a wife, a
young son and many debts. The only inheritance the son
receives is a collection of baseball cards of no interest to
him until Jonathan Hart tells him that it is worth a
fortune…..».

23. To Coin a Hart : « An expert in ancient
currencies is killed during an argument with two thugs
who steal a precious coin from him. But this one is given
to a blind flower seller, who then passes it on to Jennifer
Hart as a change….».

24. Harts and Fraud : « A small crook who has

gambling debts pushed by his lawyer and with the complicity of a crooked doctor, pretends to have an accident with Jennifer Hart to claim him two million dollars in damages. But while he is hospitalized and the Harts are brought to justice, the man is murdered by the lawyer who injects him with a lethal poison....».

In 1981, one of the episodes in the series « Hart to Hart » takes place in Hawaii. Back in Los Angeles, filming continues in Santa Monica, on the pier. Stefanie Powers takes the opportunity to see William Holden. But, despite the phone messages she leaves on her answering machine, he will never call her back.

On this Monday morning, she made her way to the film studio, when the radio announced the death of William Holden. The shock is immense for Stefanie Powers, punctuated by evidence due to the actor's alcoholic behaviour, but also given the circumstances. William Holden died a few days earlier after a blow to the head.

The forewarned friends go alongside Stefanie Powers, Natalie Wood and Robert Wagner are there. Friends arrive, enter and leave his house with their arms laden with flowers.

The funeral will be organized by the actor's family without consultation with his last partner, Stefanie Powers.

She will devote all her energy to implementing, their shared passion, the work of a lifetime: the William Holden Foundation for the Preservation of Wildlife.

Chapter 8 : And after

The first weeks after William Holden's death were difficult under the circumstances. William Holden was the love of her life. She lives in fog. She and her friends are holding a final farewell to William Holden. She returned to the studios with the support of Robert Wagner. The day after Thanksgiving, she was informed by R. McDowall that it was obviously impossible to reach Robert Wagner at his home.

Over the weekend, Natalie Wood, Robert Wagner and a friend of the couple, Christopher Walken, stayed on their yatch, the « Splendour » Catalina Island. Natalie Wood reportedly fell overboard in the night, and drowned. Her body was found the next morning by a helicopter. The news is appalling, two weeks after the death of William Holden, the companion of Stefanie

Powers, the wife of Robert Wagner, Natalie Wood dies in equally dramatic circumstances.

Robert Wagner is devastated. After her second marriage to the actress, Natalie Wood, they were one of the most fashionable couples in Los Angeles. As he said, their second marriage was different because they were well aware that their love was special and how lucky they were to bc together again. Particularly in love was a close-knit couple, parents of three children, Katie Wagner, whom the actor had had with Marion Marshall, with whom he had been married for ten years, Natacha Gregson, whom Natalie Wood had had with her ex-husband Richard Gregson and, Courtney Wagner, the daughter of Natalie Wood and Robert Wagner had together. He later met actress Jill St John, who helped him rebuild, and offered all his help and love to raise his children.

Like Stefanie Powers, Robert Wagner returns to the studios of the series « Hart to Hart ». They both find themselves in the pain of losing a loved one, their respective spouses and find solace in their fictional family in the series. He'll say later : « When Natalie died, I thought my life was over. Natalie was such a special woman, so wonderful. She'll always be with me ».

At the end of the season, Stefanie Powers goes to Africa to recharge her batteries. It creates what will become the « William Holden Wildlife Foundation » to respond to William Holden's idea of creating a wildlife training center.

Part of the ranch was separated to build the education center. Upon her return to the United States, she will continue to implement the project through the establishment of a charity to raise the necessary funds. This Foundation will be for William Holden and Stefanie Powers, the child they never had. Through this Foundation, Stefanie Powers continues the work created by her companion. It will become more important in the years to come.

Thanks to its notoriety and that generated by the success of the series « Hart to Hart », procedures for setting up the charity is facilitated. She organizes her first fundraisers for the Foundation through dinners. His close and friends are the first contributors and organizes a first big event during the organization of a polo match.

Many celebrities invited to the event play the game. It's a real success and allows her to raise $150,000. She later organized many events among her friends, Robert Wagner, William Devane, Tommy Lee Jones, Paul

Newman. All donations collected are mainly used for the Foundation.

Since its operation in 1983, more than 500,000 Kenyans have benefited from the programme at the education center. The preservation of animal species is a constant struggle. Poaching involves a large number of animals such as rhinoceros for their horns, Elephants for their tusks, Lions for their fur, each species to its poachers. The fight is unrelenting.

Iris Hunt is a long-time friend who lives in Kenya, with her husband, they invest in William Holden's project in its early days.

William Holden and Don Hunt

William Holden is back in Kenya to perform for a safari. Early in the morning, they leave and arrive at the site where a female elephant was shot. Vultures hover in a circle above it. His tusks were ripped off. The whole team is in shock. The body is riddled with thirty-seven bullet holes. The elephant was murdered for its ivory. The scene is brutal. Nearby, they find three other elephants that have also been slaughtered. They were shot at night and tire tracks are visible on the ground.

As the team struggles to regain its spirits, a shrill cry emerges. A baby elephant emerges and rushes at its mother. The little howl, William Holden and Don Hunt manage to subdue the youngster. He is frightened and must have witnessed the murder of his mother. After a lot of effort, they manage to maintain it. The shock was harsh for the trembling little animal that must now be brought back to the ranch and fed.

They reach the ranch late in the evening. The little elephant is installed on straw, warm where he will have his first meal by bottle. During the day the little elephant stays outside and starts following them all over the ranch, he is very young, three or four months at most. They managed to develop a feeding plan for the young elephant that would be named « Mary ». With a young giraffe, they become inseparable. Around the age of three, his tusks began to grow.

« Mary » has always been the star of all those who came to visit the orphanage. It was better to let her grow up on the ranch for her safety. Until suddenly, almost overnight, she had become so great that it was time for her to return to her life.

Stefanie Powers keeps her Polo ponies at the Ranch. She built her own house there. The Center continues its development in order to welcome its visitors in the best conditions and offer them the best services.

The Fairmont Mount Kenya Safari Club is a

beautiful place.

The fourth season of the series « Hart to Hart – 1982 / 1983 » includes twenty-two episodes :

1. On a Bed of Harts : « For Jennifer's birthday, Jonathan Hart offers her the bed of their honeymoon, but he confuses it with another. The couple finds the original in a hotel sold at auction, which Jonathan Hart buys on a whim. But the bed is coveted by art dealers.....».

2. With this Hart, I Thee Wed : « The Harts welcome Jennifer's aunt for her marriage to the member of a spiritual sect. But the cake of marriage, poisoned, ends the life of the groom....».

3. Million Dollars Harts : « In London, while waiting for Jonathan Hart held in a meeting, his wife Jennifer goes to the casino where she helps a baron to earn a fortune. But this one disappears, leaving the couple to leave los Angeles with the suitcase of tickets. Other people soon interested in this suitcase....».

4. Harts on Campus : « During a reunion organized by her old school, Jennifer Hart finds an old friend secretly in love with her ever. Man decides to hypnotize Jonathan Hart to get rid of him permanently.....».

5. Harts at High Noon : « Jonathan Hart is offered to save a ghost town with the backdrop of Far-West, which

serves as an attraction for tourists. The Harts decide to go there to discover the scene but witness a murder during a duel that goes wrong....».

6. <u>Harts' Desire</u> : « A former teacher of Jennifer Hart became a best-selling writer but under a female pseudonym. The author is to receive an award, he asks Jennifer Hart to pretend to be the famous novelist. But a psychopath confuses her with the character of her novels....».

7. <u>Rich and Hartless</u> : « Scammers make Max think he's made $1 million, in order to make him want to follow a new life and place two thieves as butlers at the Hart's....».

8. <u>In the Hart of the Night</u> : « A Middle Eastern king and friend of the Harts exhibits a statue very important to his people in California. But her right arm replaced her with a fake to discredit the king....».

9. <u>One Hart Too Many</u> : « Jennifer Hart investigates a fitness center and decides to spend a few days there. She discovers that her manager murders rich women and replaces them with lookalikes....».

10. <u>A Christmas Hart</u> : « The Harts are organizing Max's birthday party during which they are robbed. The flight was organized by the agency that sent two young artists to perform during the party. To confuse the culprits, Jonathan and Jennifer Hart are hired to join the

agency…».

11. <u>Hunted Harts</u> : « Irritated to lose markets to Hart, an unscrupulous industrialist decides to get rid of Jonathan Hart. To do this, he lures the couple to an African reserve to hunt it like game….».

12. <u>Emily by Hart</u> : « On a weekend in a small town on the coast, the Harts meet a young man whose fiancée, Emily, has just died. She was a young journalist who admired Jennifer. The Harts discover that she had recognized her boyfriend's boss as a fugitive drug lord…».

13. <u>Pounding Harts</u> : « The Freeway niche the Hart dog is mistakenly exchanged for another container of cocaine. In search of their drug, the thugs will do everything to recover the niche…».

14. <u>Chamber of lost Harts</u> : « The Harts go to Peru to investigate the mysterious death of a collaborator killed in the jungle by a poisoned arrow. Here they are in the footsteps of a treasure hidden by a former Inca king. But the killer slipped into the expedition team….».

15. <u>Harts on the Scent</u> : « A wealthy perfumer, who planned to sell his business to Jonathan Hart, died being attacked by his dog. After visiting the perfumery laboratory, Jonathan Hart also suffered the onslaught of his dog Freeway. The couple discovers that the industrialist's wife got rid of it using a doctored perfume

to make the dogs dangerous....».

16. <u>Bahama Bound Harts</u> : « The Harts travel to the Bahamas for a reception given by an old businessman. But Jonathan and Jennifer Hart discover that the man is dying and that the one who receives them is actually a lookalike created from scratch by his secretary in order to control his empire....».

17. <u>As the Hart Turns</u> : « During a raffle organized by the production of a soap opera, Jennifer Hart wins a role in the series. But a member of the production is found strangled, then it's the screenwriter's turn to pay the murderer's costs. Jennifer Hart is asked to write the rest of the episodes but she becomes the target of the assassin, in reality one of the actors of the show, worried about the future of his character....».

18. <u>The Waywart Hart</u> : « The Hart sover gives himself a few days to go play poker. But a little offended by the Harts who say he is too predictable, he decides to change his plans at the last moment. The next day, Jonathan and Jennifer Hart learn from the police that Max left with a poisoned cigar. Then starts a race against time to find Max before he touches the dangerous cigar....».

19. <u>A change of Hart</u> : « An architect, a friend of Jonathan Hart, must meet a politician he accuses of corruption. But a hit man infiltrates the journalists and

shoots the architect. The killer who is actually a killer runs away by jumping into Jonathan Hart's car, which she takes for the driver and finds refuge in the Harts' house. By phone, she learns that her next contract is none other than Jonathan Hart….».

20. Hartstruck : « Jonathan Hart is waiting for his wife Jennifer in a restaurant when Robin Wall, a pretty brunette spills his drink. Jonathan very gentleman offers him another, but Robin misunderstands his intentions and is inlove with the billionaire. Psychotic, the young woman pursues him with his assiduities. Things get complicated when they decide to remove anyone who stands between her and Jonathan Hart….».

21. Too close to Hart : « Max wants to invite their neighbors' housekeeper, the Sawyers, to dinner and realizes that in their absence, the house is occupied by Bill and Cheryl Hyatt. Intrigued by their behaviour, Jonathan and Jennifer Hart discover that the Hyatts, aided by a talented forger, rob the surrounding houses and replace the paintings with copies…..».

22. A Lighter Hart : « The Harts welcome Jennifer's cousin Betsy to study weight loss sessions. These are taught by Barry Grayson and his partner in their sports club. The two acolytes give their members an energy drink, Vidalite. But during a game of tennis, Betsy gets unwell and falls into a coma. Her blood test revealed that

she had abused amphetamines. Jonathan and Jennifer want to prove that Vidalite is not so harmless as Barry and his accomplice are trying to make him believe.....».

At the end of each season of the series « Hart to Hart », Stefanie Powers travels to Hong Kong to her home in Discovery Bay, but also to Kenya.

The fifth season is planning an episode that will be shot in Greece. Lionel Stander (Max), his wife and daughter travel to Europe each year and finish their trip to Rome. For his part, Robert Wagner took his daughters to Rome where he had also lived during his marriage to Marion Marshall.

Finishing filming « Family Secrets » of which she is also co-writer with Lee Thuna, she travels to Rome to see Silvano before joining Greece.

In front of all to meet in Rome on the same dates, Robert Wagner suggests that they get an audience with the Pope. Indeed, in the summer the Pope leaves Rome for his residence in Castel Gandolfo and returns to Rome on Wednesday for a public audience in St. Peter's Square.

For his part, Robert Wagner is trying to contact the American ambassador for an audience. As for Stefanie

Powers, being of Polish origin, she intends to use her contacts to overcome a possible failure of Robert Wagner.

Stefanie Powers' plane is delayed, which could jeopardize her on-time presence in St. Peter's Square. When Tom Mankiewicz and Stefanie Powers arrive at the Hassler Hotel near the Spanish Square, Lionel Stander, Robert Wagner and the girls return to the Hotel with their autographed photo in hand.

Stefanie Powers calls a Polish correspondent in Rome, Father Sokolowski. Tom Mankiewicz and Stefanie Powers will meet pope John Paul II in his residence in Castel Gondolfo for a blessing to Polish pilgrims. She will then travel to Hong Kong to her beach house in Discovery Bay. As always, her mother accompanies him and they make their trip twice a year to Hong Kong, China and Kenya.

In 1984, she co-wrote and starred in the film « Family Secrets » with Melissa Gilbert, Maureen Stapleton and James Spader. The story of three generations of women, mother, daughter and granddaughter, who meet for a weekend. Filming takes place in Los Angeles and Chicago. She will be nominated by the Writers Guild of America in the drama category, which will give her credibility as a writer and producer.

The fifth season of the series « Hart to Hart – 1983 / 1984 » includes twenty-two episodes :

1. Two Harts are better Than One ? : « On holiday in London, the Harts remember their meeting. Jonathan Hart was then in England to save a factory from bankruptcy. Harassed by a journalist named Jennifer Edwards, he becomes friends with her without knowing her job....».

2. Straight Through the Hart : « An Argentinian polo player offers his mallet to Jonathan Hart. The latter does not know that the object contains a precious stone. But when the player collapses from a heart attack, Jennifer Hart is tracked and Max is attacked in the house, the Harts understand that there is eel under rock...».

3. Hostage Hearts : « Jonathan and Jennifer Hart flew to Paris to make an offer for the acquisition of the imperial tiara that Napoleon offered to Josephine in 1809. But Jonathan Hart catches a couple of thieves stealing the precious crown....».

4. Pandora has Wings : « The Air Force is asking Jonathan Hart to test a new Pandora radar that is made of parts made by his company. But Jennifer Hart realizes

that the plane on which the mission is taking place has been sabotaged. She's going to have to save her husband, Jonathan from a planned explosion...».

5. <u>Harts and Hounds</u> : « The Harts were invited by Sir William Belgrave to a hunt for his estate in England. Upon arrival at the mansion, the couple is challenged by Lady Claire who thinks her husband is trying to kill her. But it was Sir Belgrave who died in a ball-trap....».

6. <u>Love Game</u> : « Surprised in bed by the husband of one of his clients, a tennis teacher saves her skin by delivering confidential information. In order to honor his contract, he had to extract indiscretions concerning the Hart industries. He then decides to seduce Jennifer Hart, but she discovers the double game of the seducer...».

7. <u>Passing Chance</u> : « Jonathan Hart's company is organising a charity car rally in Greece in which the Harts participate. Businessman takes advantage of this moment to launch a wild takeover bid for Hart Industries and take over the company....».

8. <u>Long lost Love</u> : « Jennifer Hart's father meets a young woman whose mother was her great love during the Second World War. Under the influence of her lover, she pretends to be Steven Edwards' natural daughter in order to recover part of her fortune....».

9. <u>Highland Fling</u> : « Because of her Scottish origins, Jennifer Hart is designated by a clan as heir to a

castle. But the property contains a treasure a royal sword, an object as historic as it is precious. A rich Scottish man is determined to get his hands on this sword even if he has to remove the Harts...».

10. Year of The Dog : « Jonathan Hart offers his wife, Jennifer the famous « Dog of Jade », a precious jewel. Legend has it that the person who detains the twelve Jade animals of the Emperor of China is invulnerable...».

11. Trust Your Hart : « Lisa, a young girl of the Harts, is coming out of a seven-year coma. Jonathan and Jennifer Hart welcome convalescent with failing memory home....».

12. Harts on The Run : « Jennifer Hart is witnessing a murderous settlement involving a wealthy businessman. Poorly protected by the police, it narrowly escapes an attack. Jonathan Hart decides to shelter her and after a clever diversion, the couple finds refuge in a monastery disguised as religious....».

13. Whispers in the Wings : « The Harts attend a charity gala in New York where they rehearse a musical performance. But an unbalanced theater that haunts old stage manager confuses Jennifer Hart with an actress he murdered six years earlier....».

14. Max 'Waltz : « Max has a romance with Catherine, a wealthy widow with whom he dances in a

club. But an alleged businessman charms the lady in order to extract a fortune from her…..».

15. The Dog Who Knew Too Much : « During a dog show, a man chased entrusts his dog to the Harts. They have no doubt that the animal carries in it a very important genetic formula and that they have put their finger in a dark case of industrial espionage….».

16. Silence Dance : « Jonathan and Jennifer Hart help Susan, a young skater who became deaf after a car accident. With a hearing aid, she resumes training, but with the Harts, she is the subject of several assaults….».

17. Death Dig : « During a cruise to Greece on their sailboat, Jonathan and Jennifer Hart meet in Rhodes a prominent professor who investigates the looting of an archaeological site. As police sue the Harts for holding a national historic statue on their boat, the couple must find their old friend, captured by the criminals….».

18. The Shooting : « The Harts decided to spend a few days on their ranch, where an advertisement for one of Jonathan Hart's companies was shot. The capricious director flashes on Jennifer Hart and asks her to take the lead…..».

20. Larsen's Last Jump : « Jonathan and Jennifer Hart receive a couple of friends, Richard and Pamela, to watch the film of their last snow vacation. The camera filmed a hooded man sabotaging skis….».

21. <u>Always, Elizabeth</u> : « Max has a correspondence with a wealthy New Yorker. When she announces that he is coming to Los Angeles, Max panics: he makes her think he's also a millionaire. The Harts decide to play the game and propose to become the servants of the house, the time of stay....».

22. <u>Meanwhile, Back at the Ranch</u> : « Returning from vacation earlier than expected, the Harts discover that their home is occupied by a group of criminals who are preparing a jewelry theft. The thugs are waiting for the arrival of the lookalikes of the two billionaires to perfect their combine....».

The fifth season ends, the coast of the series has dropped slightly, but the audience remains perfectly correct. For the sixth season, Robert Wagner wants to shoot two episodes in France. One will take place in the fashion industry, and the second will feature a love story between a dog and Freeway.

Being already in France for the series « <u>Mistral's Daughter</u> » with Stacy Keach and Lee Remick, as Maggie Lunel, the broadcast channel (ABC) announces to the production, that the series « <u>Hart to Hart</u> » will not be renewed for a sixth season.

It was the three producers, Robert Wagner, Mankiewicz and Leonard, who informed him. It was a shock to the whole team.

During these five years, the series « Hart to Hart » ensuring everyone the comfort each morning to go to the filming locations of the series within what had become for all « their family ». The series has been a real success all these years and continues to generate interest today. If she had not been arrested, she could have continued for several more years. Scenarios for the sixth season were ready.

Stefanie Powers was particularly upset by the sudden shutdown. As she herself will say : « This was decided at the last moment, the first four scripts were ready, the production unit was in Paris ready to start filming, it was a real shock ».

When Robert Wagner calls her to Paris to tell her, she bursts into tears. The teams had worked a lot on the scripts and they were all looking forward to starting this new season. As she will say : « Robert Wagner is my boyfriend, and none of us spent so much time with another man or woman or child and the financial blow was a shock too ». Moreover, they both regretted not saying goodbye to the series.

She remembers during a visit to Rome that a woman called her « Jennifer » recognizing her. On the other hand, she acknowledges that often people who have worked on a series say it was a big family. It considers that this was quite the case with the series « Hart to Hart ». Robert Wagner was wonderful, she said, and we were happy to do this series. This series is for her the happiest years of her professional career.

Her character « Jennifer Hart » is very interesting. Her personality to a certain extent is quite close to hers and she is totally committed to her role. « She is an independent woman with a professional career », she said. « Couple Jennifer and Jonathan Hart have a relationship based on complicity and they may have disagreements during a conversation.

It is not a juvenile relationship, but an adult relationship. They were a married couple and a true role model for many people all over the world. Jennifer Hart being a modern woman and who always puts her husband first in her life. With Robert Wagner, we played a married couple, very rich, very sophisticated and very human. They always have something to do around the world and rub shoulders with danger and crime. In addition, in their roles, they often have to improvise, which is part of the role of an actor». As Robert Wagner will say, « We had a lot of fun working together. We have traveled to many places and brought a lot of ourselves into our characters. I've never had such a great working relationship with someone else before ».

This five- or six-year working relationship has created a very close relationship. « I really like Stefanie, she makes me laugh and she has a great mind, she is a very interesting woman. We have never been involved together in a romantic relationship, but we are very good friends », he said.

In fact, in an interview with Larry King in 2002 :

LK : A lot of people thought who you were married to.

RW : Yes, but we had working on a series together and we appreciate each other. And when casting for the role of Jennifer Hart, I didn't want another actress to play the role of my wife in the series.

In terms of the role of « Jonathan Hart », Stefanie Powers admits that the chemistry between them wouldn't have worked if they hadn't been friends. « He's professional and a true gentleman. And only he was able to play that role », she said.

In a 1996 interview with Mike and Maty, Robert Wagner explained that he met Stephanie Powers on the set of « West Side Story ». Stefanie Powers explained that she had passed seven dance auditions and three on-screen tests and had performed rehearsals for several months. But at the time, she was only fifteen years old and the Youth Work Act did not allow her to work. The production finally had to choose another girl for the role. She had an extraordinary opportunity to work with Jerome Robbins and the dancers and Natalie Wood starred in a beautiful film. « This film was great, but it's true that a good thing you happened at that moment, robert Wagner will say.

Yes, a very good thing, she will answer.

Yes, a very good thing, says Robert Wagner, because it's a great story that's going to happen in her career.

You know I was engaged, says SP, I had done tests for an independent, a producer director writer, it was at Sam, at the Goldwyn studio here in Hollywood and he liked working with people who didn't have much experience because he wanted shape and shape them in his own image. He came and looked at that test I was doing. Then later, he asked me to go read a text. I read the text and he hired me. Then several studios asked me to come and participate in their programs.

I think it was Tom Laughlin, said Robert Wagner.

Yes, and Billy Jack, adds Stefanie Powers, they had an amazing program and fabulous teachers.

You know, says RW, in this business you never know what's going to happen, you meet someone and he tells you, hold on I have a role for you and it's just great when that happens to you.

In an episode of the sequel to the series « Hart to Hart », Stefanie Powers held a koala in her arms.

Stefanie was very comfortable with animals, says Robert Wagner. She's exceptionally good with them. I was very nervous because the last time she held a koala in her arms, there was an incident. We were in San Diego, playing theater for « Love Letters » and we went to the exhibition in the zoo. They had just received a koala. Stefanie holds him in her arms and the photographers take pictures, and then all of a sudden she's left with a bloody chin.

Their nails are so sharp says Stefanie Powers, that since I've learned to hold their paws firmly in my hands because they want and it's natural, cling ingon and that's how they feel safe. He just touched my cheek, but his nails made a long cut and blood was pouring down my cheek.

During these years of filming, they shared many together with the whole team and celebrated their birthdays on the set. The challenge was each time to find something more elaborate.

On a birthday of Stefanie, says Robert Wagner, we opened the door very gently of his dressing room, and brought in an Ourang-Outan. When she saw the animal while she was wearing make-up, her heart almost stopped.

You set up the William Holden Foundation after his death, it's good for you to take care of these things in Kenya..

We first realized his desire to build a youth education centre for the preservation of Kenya's wildlife, so that people can learn more about this very precious natural resource that they have what they have Have. It is essential that they understand the preservation of these species. We have about 3,000 students a year in our centre in Kenya and we have had groups of students from abroad who have come on some kind of exchange program. They come to our seminar that we are conducting in August from five to ten days, says Stefanie Powers.

She's doing a great job, says Robert Wagner.

At the end of the filming of « Mistral's Daughter », she moved to London with her mother to meet her friends, then returned to Kenya. It was during this stay that Stefanie Powers was contacted by Aaron Spelberg to play in « Hollywood Wives », based on the novel by Joan Collins, starring Antony Perkins, Roddy McDowall, Angie Dickinson, Joanna Cassidy and Candice Bergen.

She then toured a mini-series entitled « <u>Deceptions</u> » in 1985, with Barry Bostwick on NBC where she played the dual role of Sabrina and Stephanie : « Between a husband who abandons her and her two children, Stephanie is tired of this monotonous life. She envy the existence of her twin sister, Sabrina, who runs an art gallery in London. The two sisters decide to exchange their lives for a week. A game that will quickly prove dangerous ».

In 1986, she worked on multiple projects for CBS. Ted Turner is in negotiations for the CBS takeover. At a party in Washington for Jacques-Yves Cousteau's 75th birthday, Ted Turner says he wants to buy CBS so he can work with Stefanie Powers.

During the last season of the « <u>Hart to Hart</u> », she is contacted to appear in advertisements. It was an opportunity to provide additional funds for the William Holden Foundation.

She advertises for makeup « Cover Girl », « London Fog » and the magazine « Sears » for the cover of their catalogue. The latter was considering producing a line of women's clothing and the « <u>Stefanie Collection</u> ». It was distributed in nearly seven hundred stores, for a total of nearly 64,000 pieces for the collections, or two collections per year for the next five years. Spitalnick and Co. was in charge of the design of the line, which was distributed locally in department stores « Sears » December 1985 and in the spring-summer 1986 collection catalogue.

She was contacted by Alexander Cohen, a Broadway producer, to appear in a television show called « The night of the 100 stars » alongside Placido Domingo with whom she will perform a song. This experience rekindles his passion for musical theatre. Alexander Cohen offers to sing dance for a show for Tony Award TV.

In 1988, she shot in the TV movie « The Shadow on the sun » by Tony Richardson. She plays the role of Beryl Markham, a woman of many talents : aviator, horse breeder, writer, adventurer.

With a friend, Judy Balaban involved in the world of sports and especially fitness, she created a book « Superlife » containing exercises, photos, which will be followed by a second work of exercises based on techniques « Pilates » published by Simon & Schuster.

For the holiday season, Stefanie Powers and her mother are both flying to Nepal. Their first steps are New Delhi where they will visit the « Lal Quila ».

Listed as a UNESCO World Heritage Site in 2007, it takes its name from the red sandstone that covers the entire fortress and its 2 km long walls. It was built between 1638 and 1648 by Shah Jahan, the Mongol Emperor who built the Taj Mahal for his late wife. The entrance through the Lahore Gate was added to the fort by Shah Jahan's son to hide it from the sight of the people of Delhi.

A commercial gallery was intended to supply the fort, which had a piece called « Naubat Khana » intended for the Emperor's musicians. It has a museum of independence fighters from India. Then the emperor's private apartments, whose elements of refined marble decorations, gilding and sculptures remain, and finally the Pearl Mosque with its three marble domes.

They join Chitwan National Park and stay in at the Tiger Tops Hotel. Built of bamboo, the walls are a woven grass carpet. Solar panels heat the water for the rooms. The whole thing is quite rustic. Her mother is seventy-nine years old and is always happy to travel. They reach New Delhi where they are expected by the family of the owners of the Oberoi Hotel, who know William Holden from the time of the filming of the film « The Bridge of the River Kwai ».

They also visit the Taj Mahal. Located in Agra, on the banks of the Yamunâ River, it is a white marble mausoleum built by the Mughal emperor Shâh Jahân in memory of his wife Arjumand Bânu Begam, also known as the « *Mumtaz Mahal* », which means in Persian « the light of the palace ».

She died giving birth to her fourteenth child, when she had already lost eight. The Taj Mahal was built using materials from various parts of India and the rest of Asia. More than 1,000 elephants were used to transport building materials during construction. Twenty-eight types of fine or ornamental stones were used to compose the marquetry patterns encrusted in white marble.

The central dome of the tomb is surrounded by four identical minarets, which tilt outwards. In the event of an earthquake, they would collapse in the opposite direction to the tomb.

It is on the occasion of their return flight to Europe that they stop in Frankfurt for their connection with England. The aircraft that was to land had been delayed, it was the PAN AM 103 flight that one of their friends had taken. It crashed over Lockerbie.

Back in the United States, American industry underwent many changes, with the rise of Wall Street and globalization. Hollywood is also continuing its development. The studios are bought by larger firms with greater financial resources.

Stefanie Powers continues her career even if the projects proposed to her are less interesting. The William Holden Foundation's Education Centre continues to develop. It has an amphitheatre and a library with hundreds of books and videos. The reputation of the centre is growing in popularity and many students benefit from the teachings.

More than 500,000 Kenyan and adult students benefit from the curriculum and libraries built in primary and secondary schools in rural communities. They have maps, books and information on the environment and wildlife. The center produces solar energy, water recycling. Conferences are set up for groups for one day or more.

At the same time, Stefanie Powers obtained a board position at the Los Angeles Zoo. She is invited to the cincinnati and Atlanta councils. In Cincinnati, Professor B. Dresser introduces him to the use of freezing methods « cryonic » for the conservation of flora and fauna.

This process preserves DNA, tissues, and sperm to ensure the conservation of species. The same is true of embryo research and the transfer of one of them from an antelope. The last group of antelopes « Bongo » is located at the Mount Kenya Wildlife Conservatory, many of which had been captured by William Holden at the creation of their Ranch.

She participated in expeditions, including one with Dr. T. Maple, Director of the Atlanta Zoo, on the island of Sumatra, to study flora and fauna on the Awash River and in the rainforest. When they return, they will make a documentary.

For the BBC, she will travel to Alaska to rub shoulders with bears, white-headed eagles and salmon for a « Safari World ».

In 1993, she took part in the feature film « Survive the night ». On the way back from Brooklyn psychiatrist Victoria (Stefanie), daughter Julie and sister Stacey runs gas. They leave the freeway to look for a gas station, but end up losing in the South Bronx. A gang of youths under the sadistic ice stops their car and starts threatening them. When Julie leaves in a panic, she damages one of their bikes. The ice feels provoked and decides to track them down. Without fuel the three women must soon flee on foot and defend their lives with all possible means. Only the youngest member of the T.J. gang is trying to help them. The film also starred with Helen Shaver and Peter MacNeil.

Chapter 9 : Love Letters

In an interview, Stefanie Powers said that she and Robert Wagner had wanted to work together again since the end of the tv series « Hart to Hart », in which they played a couple of millionaires, globetrotters adventurers, and crime-solving enthusiasts. This series, which lasted six years, left them many wonderful memories, not only because of the atmosphere of the shoot, but also because of their mutual complicity.

In 1990, a successful play at the Steppenwolf Theatre recounted the relationship of two people of forty years, both friends and occasional lovers. It was a very popular show, because of its location, the reading of letters.

Reading these letters, it seems natural for Robert

Wagner to interpret these letters with Stefanie Powers. Their rehearsals begin in the actor's Brentwood residence in front of a group of friends. Both have not played theatre for many years, so it seemed obvious to them to practice in front of an audience reduced to the essentials.

Nearly seven years after the end of the series « Hart to Hart », contact was immediately made between them, and after a day of rehearsal, the premiere took place at the Wilbur Theatre in Boston. The end of this premiere ended with a standing ovation from the audience. The next day, one of their friend, Robert Osborne, wrote in the « Hollywood Reporter » that they had broken all records in a single evening of a week of hearings at the Wilbur Theatre. These performances were the beginning of a long series.

They crisscrossed the country, went to Canada, Hawaii, London. Everywhere the reception was amazing. Meet on stage the couple « Hart » was an extraordinary moment for the audience, who remained faithfully in love with Jennifer and Jonathan Hart.

In January 1991, they began a five-week tour of Seattle in front of a room of twenty-seven thousand people. The room is huge and despite their concern about this room, the show is successful. They had a standing ovation. At the same time, it was during that night that the Gulf War was launched. They return to their hotel to see the information on CNN. The next day, they received the same welcome at the theatre and signed autographs.

In 1991, Still on tour, Stefanie Powers received an offer from a friend, Bryon Morrison, who offered her a musical play called « Matador ». She moved to London, Kensington in the house lent to her by a friend. Her mother joined her for the first performance, as did her lawyer Leo Ziffren. Her mother had health problems six months earlier. When she returns to Kensington, she realizes that her mother is not as usual. She assures her that she will consult as soon as she returns to Los Angeles. Unfortunately, the play does not receive the expected success and the performances will not go beyond three months.

A friend wants to introduce him to an acquaintance, he is French and is called : Patrick Houtte de la Chesnais. He attends one of the performances of « Matador » and must show up at his dressing room. It was when she returned home that she received a call informing her of the arrival of a last visitor. She discovers this tall, brown man with a charming smile. A few days later, she receives flowers accompanied by a note inviting her to a Polo tournament in her property.

Patrick de la Chesnais owns a huge property near the Swiss border, in the heart of Beaujolais. Wooded grounds, two polo fields, an equestrian centre and a golf course with a neo-Gothic castle from 1823. His noble family has many castles, most of which require extensive repairs.

Divorced and father of two daughters, he is attractive and their attraction is mutual. The last ten years following William Holden's death have put his life on hold, and it may be time to try again to be happy.

After their marriage in Kenya, they moved to England. Unfortunately, the complexity of their lives and their professional demands does not allow them to build a viable relationship that ends in divorce six years later.

Chapter 10 : « Hart to Hart »

While continuing their tour with the « <u>Love Letters</u> », NBC would like to offer them a sequel to the series « <u>Hart to Hart</u> », but in the form of four two-hour episodes. It is a new concept that was developed in the 1970s by Universal Television. They agreed to a five-episode series with new producers and having Robert Wagner as executive producer.

After the fifth episode, Lionel Stander, who played the character of « Max » in the series, dies. As an integral part of this series since the beginning of its concept, it seems inconceivable to the actors to continue. This fifth episode will have a day of filming organized in New York due to the appearance of Donald Trump.

Robert Wagner and Stefanie continue their

performances at the « <u>Love Letters</u> », two of which were given in Las Vegas.

Telefilm « <u>Hart to Hart</u> » - 1993 / 1996 :

1. <u>Hart to Hart Returns</u> – 1993 : « Jonathan Hart reflects on the gift he'll give his wife Jennifer for his birthday ».

This is the first of the TV movies « Hart à Hart » and the one where their house burns down, because their original home had been destroyed when the TV series was stopped.

2. <u>Home is Where the Hart is</u> – 1994 : « When Jennifer Hart's beloved teacher and mentor suddenly dies, she leaves the town she owned, the Kingman Ferry, to Jennifer. A trail of mysterious clues leads the Harts to long-guard secrets about the city that directly attach themselves to his friend's "accident" and it seems that the Harts are destined to respond to the same fate unless they can solve the mystery before it be too late ».

3. <u>Crimes of the Hart</u> – 1994 : « Someone is trying to sabotage a Broadway production of a play Jennifer Hart wrote at the University. When one of the stage hands is murdered, even Jonathan Hart is a suspect. The

Harts don't have much time to make sure the show will continue ».

4. <u>Old Friends Never Die</u> – 1994 : « Jonathan and Jennifer Hart travel to publisher Alfred Raines' private island for a party that Raines hopes to get Jennifer Hart to sign a publishing contract. When Jennifer hears someone plotting to murder a man over the weekend, she and Jonathan discover that someone is trying to kill them ».

5. <u>Secrets of the Hart</u> – 1995 : « While at a Hart Industries charity auction, Jennifer Hart finds a medallion that could hold the key to unlock Jonathan Hart's early years spent at the Mission Street Orphanage and the family he never knew ».

6. <u>Two Harts in Three Quarter Time</u> – 1995 : « When the Harts accept a clock left for them by Max, their recently deceased butler, he becomes the centerpiece of a case involving blackmail and murder ».

7. <u>Harts in High Season</u> – 1996 : « The Harts travel to Australia to buy a wildlife reserve from former Jennifer Hart lover Elliott Manning (James Brolin). Believing that Jonathan Hart stole Jennifer from him,

Manning plots to fake his own death....».

8. <u>Till Death Do Us Hart</u> – 1996 : « The Harts go to Munich where Jennifer Hart is a bone marrow donor for a little boy who has leukemia. The doctor is surprised by Jennifer Hart's looks with his fiancee.. ».

It was during a night out at a friend's house that she met Tomas Carroll. A few years earlier, a psychic had informed her that she would meet a cowboy with a hat, and that was Tom Carroll. A sportsman, he was a fan of the New York City Marathon that he did every year.

Tomas Carroll is a graduate of the University of Notre Dame and is a former U.S. Navy Officer. Early in his career, he became a CPA and joined KPMG.

As a member of the New York Yacht Club and the Larchmont Yacht Club, he continued his passion for sailing with great success and reward as captain of « Siren Song ». He ran nine New York City marathons and finished once in less than four hours.

He established the Patrick and Mary Carroll Scholarship Fund at the University of Notre Dame and served on the Board of Directors of the William Holden Wildlife Foundation. He died in 2014.

She's on her way to New York. As soon as she arrives at the airport, she receives a message to call back her home. Her mother fell and fractured her hip, she is at Cedars Sinai Hospital where she is reunited with her sister, Aunt Helena, who fractured her hip the night before. She returned the next day to Los Angeles with Tom Carroll.

His mother and sister finish their recovery in a nursing home. Her aunt Helena died at the age of 92.

In June 2007, while on a cruise with Tom Carroll off sicily, the Captain of the Board informed her that she had to recall her home. Her mother has pneumonia and was admitted to intensive care.

They returned to California after making stops in Palermo, Rome, New York and finally Los Angeles after twenty-six hours of travel. Her mom's practically in a coma. After a puncture of her lungs, she finds her the next morning having breakfast in her room. She left the hospital a week later after a feeding tube was placed.

They celebrate July 21, 2007, his eighty-forewar anniversary surrounded by nearly twenty-five friends.

In the summer of 2008, Stefani Powers went to England. Her mother's condition is stable, and the medical team set up provides daily care. She begins rehearsals for a musical. Her doctor contacted her and wants her to have a ct scan of the lungs. She's going back to Los Angeles to do X-rays. The results are unmistakable, she must undergo the removal of the upper lobe of the right lung. She has lung cancer.

Together with Tom Carroll, they decide to consult and have a second opinion. On her way to England, she stopped in New York. The diagnosis is confirmed. She returns to Los Angeles where her operation is scheduled for January 29.

On Boxing Day, her mom gets a cold. She's put on antibiotics and goes home. After 24 hours, her condition deteriorates. The infection has reached her lungs.

Stefanie Powers has two shows on December 31st, she will return to Los Angeles at the end of the two performances.

When she arrives at the hospital, she enters her room and finds her mother with her eyes open waiting for her. The next day, doctors informed her that unfortunately her condition could not improve. He was given morphine for the next two days.

On December 31, 2008, Stefanie Powers' mother died at the age of 96, and on January 29, 2009, Stefanie

Powers underwent surgery for lung cancer.

Chapter 11 : Stefanie Powers, today

Sport is omnipresent in the life of the actress. From an early age, she was enrolled in classical dance classes. This discipline will serve her throughout her life.

In several episodes of the series « Hart to Hart », she participates in dance sessions in a direct or indirect way. She also practices gymnastics.

She is interested in the Pilates method she practices on a daily basis. Working with classic Pilates, Stefanie Powers has developed the perfect wellness and fitness solution for the over fifty. Its program integrates traditional Pilates with innovative movement patterns, to work the body as a whole, giving leaner, stronger and more efficient muscles. She is the author of several books « Powers Pilates »

Passionate about Polo, which she has practiced for many years, she participates in many polo matches, and is part of the team in England.

At a Polo event, held on a Sunday afternoon, Robert Wagner declined to participate in the match due to back pain following the recording of one of the episodes of the series « Hart to Hart » two days earlier. Later in the day, he will present him with the Winners' Trophy.

Stefanie Powers, who led her team on the field, lost the match 3-2. Nevertheless, this event raises $130,000 for the William Holden Foundation.

She regularly plays polo matches and is a member of the Palm Beach International Polo Club in Miami, Florida, and participates in numerous event matches.

She also participates in Cartier International Day and is a member of the Royal Country Berkshire Polo Club in England.

The Foundation's charity events are held in Palm Springs and Palm Beach, Florida, even Los Angeles remains a fundamental place of organization.

Food

She began her interest in a healthy lifestyle from an

early age. Today, she continues to travel the world on behalf of wildlife conservation, create projects for her production company, and speak for the many causes that are vitally important to her foundation.

Stefanie Powers grew up on a ranch in California, close to horses and many animals. A life close to nature. Her basic diet is semi-vegetarian, and complements her vitamin diet. Her diet has always been preserved from sugar and sodas. She does not eat bread, and has a diet based on vegetables and protein.

In Kenya, she grows her own vegetables and is currently building a greenhouse to grow tomatoes. Because of the altitude, she has to buy fruit, but raises her own chickens and composts her. She tries to lead a balanced life and eliminates processed foods from her diet. She adds multi-vitamins, flaxseed oil to her diet.

Stefanie Powers' career has spanned more than half a century. Her lifelong commitment to making the world a better place has led to his involvement in many public charities, and in her work to save endangered species.

She is not only a proponent of wildlife outside the United States, however. She is a member of the Los Angeles Zoo and a regular speaker on all kinds of animal issues in this country. Her love of wildlife extends to pets.

Her most famous character and the one who is more often in the memoirs, remains that of Jennifer Hart in the series « Hart to Hart » with Robert Wagner who for more than five years for which she earned five Emmy nominations.

Today

Even today, Stefanie Powers is very active in her charitable foundations. She continues her Polo performances, continues her dance classes three times a week.

She has gone through a lot of upand and down in her private life, fought the disease, and is always positive, which is for her the key to success. She has not had a child, but is a fulfilled godmother and is delighted that one of William Holden's granddaughters has joined her on the Board of Directors of the Wildlife Foundation.

Having a residency in London, she visits regularly and has recently performed on the British stage, at the Cambridge Arts Theatre.

In 2014, she starred in the film for television « Ring

by Spring ».

It has its own production company and continues its involvement in various animal defense programs, such as the preservation of Jaguars in Guatemala and Costa Rica..

It is very active in all environmental programs and in the manufacture of recycled products and materials. She participates in the boards of several zoos, and writes books on fitness programs (Pilates). She shares her home with her pets.

The Foundation celebrated its 20th anniversary and receives more than 70,000 visitors and some 10,000 students a year.

Nominations :

For her role as Jennifer Hart, Stefanie Powers received two Emmy nominations for Best Television Actress, and five Golden Globe Award nominations as Best Television Actress.

In 1992, she received her star on the Hollywood Walk of Fame at 6776 Hollywood Boulevard, in the category « Television ».

She received the Sarah Siddons Award in 1993 for her stage performance in Love Letters.

On March 12, 2011, she was awarded the Steiger Prize (Germany) for her achievement in the arts.

On November 6, 2017, she was honored by the women of Palm Springs in the film Television Organization (PSWIFT) with the "9th Annual Glass Break Award" for her work as an actress, author and animal advocate.

La classe de ballet avec Natalie Wood, Jill St John et Stefanie Powers.

Audition « West Side Story – 1957

« Les Internes » en 1962

« Les dingues sont lâchés » en 1963

« Le grand Mc Lintock » en 1963

« Fanatic » en 1965

« La Diligence vers l'Ouest » en 1966

« Annie, Agent très Spécial » en 1967

« Opération Vol » en 1970 avec Robert Wagner

« Un nouvel amour de Coccinelle » en 1974

« Gone with the West » en 1975

« The man inside » en 1976

« Bons baisers d'Athènes » en 1979

La série "Pour l'amour du risqué" (Hart to Hart) de 1979 à 1984.

« Secrets de Famille » en 1984

« L'amour en Héritage » en 1984

« Prête-moi ta Vie » en 1985

En 1988, dans le téléfilm : « L'aventurière du bout du monde »

Les téléfilms hors saison – Hart to Hart 1993 à 1996

(Hors saison 1 - Hart to Hart : Returns - 1993)

(Hors saison 2 – Hart to Hart : Home is where the Hart is – 1994)

(Hors saison 3 – Hart to Hart : Old Friends Never Die – 1994)

(Hors saison 4 – Hart to Hart : Crime of the Hart – 1994)

(Hors saison 5 – Hart to Hart : Two Harts in Three Quarter Time – 1995)

(Hors saison 6 – Hart to Hart : Secrets of the Hart – 1995)

(Hors saison 7 – Till Death Do Us Hart" - 1996

(Hors saison 8 – Harts in High Season – 1996)

Stefanie Powers et Robert Wagner au Théâtre

« Les Lettres d'Amour » au Théâtre avec Robert Wagner

Le couple Natalie Wood et Robert Wagner

Stefanie Powers et son mari Gary Lockwood

William Holden

Stefanie Powers et William Holden

William Holden et Grace Kelly / Avec Audrey Hepburn

Voyage en Inde

Le Fort Rouge au Népal

Le Taj Mahal - Inde

Stefanie Powers au Kenya

Stefanie Powers, joueuse de Polo

Stefanie Powers, son mariage avec Patrick Houitte de la Chesnais

Stefanie Powers et Tomas Carroll

Les récompenses

Sarah Sidon Awards   Hollywood Walk on Fame

A class of acting students

Printed in Great Britain
by Amazon

34141809R00104